A TENNYSON CHRONOLOGY

Macmillan Author Chronologies

General Editor: Norman Page, Professor of Modern English Literature, University of Nottingham

Reginald Berry
A POPE CHRONOLOGY

Edward Bishop
A VIRGINIA WOOLF CHRONOLOGY

Timothy Hands
A GEORGE ELIOT CHRONOLOGY

Owen Knowles
A CONRAD CHRONOLOGY

Harold Orel
A KIPLING CHRONOLOGY

Norman Page
A BYRON CHRONOLOGY
A DICKENS CHRONOLOGY
A DR JOHNSON CHRONOLOGY

F. B. Pinion
A WORDSWORTH CHRONOLOGY
A TENNYSON CHRONOLOGY

R. C. Terry
A TROLLOPE CHRONOLOGY

Further titles in preparation

A Tennyson Chronology

F. B. PINION
formerly Reader in English Studies
University of Sheffield

MACMILLAN

First published 1990

Published by
THE MACMILLAN PRESS LTD
Houndmills, Basingstoke, Hampshire RG21 2XS
and London
Companies and representatives
throughout the world

Printed and bound in Great Britain at
The Camelot Press plc, Southampton

British Library Cataloguing in Publication Data
Pinion, F. B. (Francis, Bertram,) *1908–*
A Tennyson chronology. — (Macmillan author chronologies)
1. Poetry in English. Tennyson,
Alfred Tennyson, Baron, 1809–1892
I. Title
821′.8
ISBN 0–333–46020–0

Contents

List of Abbreviations

Initials are used wherever the text makes their significance clear. Except where forenames are appropriate, the following abbreviations are used more consistently:

AH	Arthur Henry Hallam
ET	Emily Tennyson (*née* Sellwood)
Fitz	Edward FitzGerald
JS	James Spedding
RB	Robert Browning
T	Tennyson; Alfred Tennyson
WA	William Allingham

General Editor's Preface

Most biographies are ill adapted to serve as works of reference – not surprisingly so, since the biographer is likely to regard his function as the devising of a continuous and readable narrative, with excursions into interpretation and speculation, rather than a bald recital of facts. There are times, however, when anyone reading for business or pleasure needs to check a point quickly or to obtain a rapid overview of part of an author's life or career; and at such moments turning over the pages of a biography can be a time-consuming and frustrating occupation. The present series of volumes aims at providing a means whereby the chronological facts of an author's life and career, rather than needing to be prised out of the narrative in which they are (if they appear at all) securely embedded, can be seen at a glance. Moreover, whereas biographies are often, and quite understandably, vague over matters of fact (since it makes for tediousness to be forever enumerating details of dates and places), a chronology can be precise whenever it is possible to be precise.

Thanks to the survival, sometimes in very large quantities, of letters, diaries, notebooks and other documents, as well as to thoroughly researched biographies and bibliographies, this material now exists in abundance for many major authors. In the case of, for example, Dickens, we can often ascertain what he was doing in each month and week, and almost on each day, of his prodigiously active working life; and the student of, say, *David Copperfield* is likely to find it fascinating as well as useful to know just when Dickens was at work on each part of that novel, what other literary enterprises he was engaged in at the same time, whom he was meeting, what places he was visiting, and what were the relevant circumstances of his personal and professional life. Such a chronology is not, of course, a substitute for a biography; but its arrangement, in combination with its index, makes it a much more convenient tool for this kind of purpose; and it may be acceptable as a form of 'alternative' biography, with its own distinctive advantages as well as its obvious limitations.

Since information relating to an author's early years is usually scanty and chronologically imprecise, the opening section of some volumes in this series groups together the years of childhood and adolescence. Thereafter each year, and usually each month, is dealt with separately. Information not readily assignable to a specific month or day is given as a general note under the relevant year or month. The first entry for each month carries an indication of the day of the week, so that when necessary this can be readily calculated for other dates. Each volume also contains a bibliography of the principal sources of information. In the chronology itself the sources of many of the more specific items, including quotations, are identified, in order that the reader who wishes to do so may consult the original contexts.

NORMAN PAGE

Introduction

The principal sources for this work are given in the Bibliography. To comment on their comparative merits would be invidious and perhaps supererogatory; one does not have to research far into Tennysonian biography to realize what a difficult chronological field one has entered. Cecil Y. Lang and Edgar F. Shannon's edition of the Tennyson letters has provided much valuable information and guidance, and it is a source of regret that their third volume has not been published in time to contribute to the entries from 1871 onwards. To expand these I have consulted a large selection of letters at the Tennyson Research Centre, Lincoln; and I am especially indebted to Miss Susan Gates for her help and advice in making these available, and in answering questions on difficulties which have arisen. I am grateful also to other members of the Lincoln Central Reference Library who have assisted, and, for conclusive evidence on two items, to Elizabeth Bews and Jean Archibald of the University of Edinburgh, and Ann Duncan of the University Registry, Cambridge.

As could be expected of a famous nineteenth-century author who reached his eighty-fourth year, and retained many friends of distinction, Tennyson's life affords ample material for a biographer. Yet, for a chronologist who wishes to provide continuity of interest without allowing his presentation to remain disproportionately meagre or become excessively inclusive at particular junctures, it is surprisingly fraught with difficulties. There are periods, especially in the unsettled years before his marriage, when we know little of Tennyson's activities, or even, at times, of his whereabouts. There is little evidence once again much later in his life, when he was preoccupied with historical research and the writing of full-length plays. Tennyson rarely wrote letters of great length; most of the time he had a strong disinclination to correspond, even with friends. He lost touch with Coventry Patmore for many years through his failure to reply; continual failure of this kind induced Edward FitzGerald to write to Emily Tennyson, but, knowing how burdened she was with her husband's correspondence, he usually wrote to her about twice a year only. Tennyson's aversion was due undoubtedly to poor eyesight (a handicap which normally did not dissuade him from continual reading); it arose more, one suspects, from the musing introspection and indolence of his genius.

When his letters are undated (as is found not infrequently) they can sometimes be placed in their chronological context by internal evidence, and even more definitely when precise external evidence is found in the correspondence or records of friends or contemporaries. The dates of some remain so uncertain that they are best dismissed from chronological reckoning. Some letters may survive only as copies, sometimes with conjectural dates; dates may occasionally have been misread in copying. One transcription in an unknown hand gives 4 March 1889 for a letter in which Tennyson thanks Charles Merivale for a translation which had arrived that morning; he is very blind, he adds, but would be glad to see his old friend. Reference to Merivale's letter of 3 March 1869 suggests a probable error of twenty years.

Though Tennyson was active in many ways, and far from neglectful of his family interests, his bookishness and creative brooding demanded his continual withdrawal into a world of his own. For his benefit Emily kept her journal, and wrote increasingly to his correspondents, until she broke down; to replace her secretarially, Hallam was withdrawn from Cambridge before he could take a degree. Acting for many years as his father's correspondent and representative, he was in an advantageous position for compiling the massive memoir of Tennyson which he completed in 1896, with the assistance of his mother. Much of this biography depends on her journal, sometimes on records kept by Tennyson himself, as well as on a generous selection from his correspondence. Sometimes the dating of letters is Hallam's; too often it is inaccurate, occasionally by a year or two. Tennyson's letter to Mrs Brookfield, on the death of her husband (his old Cambridge friend) is dated January 1874 instead of July; another, referring to Swinburne's *Atalanta in Calydon*, is given under 1863 instead of 1865, the year of its publication. Yet the chronologist is glad to return to *Alfred Lord Tennyson: A Memoir*, knowing that it contains valuable evidence and sequences which are not to be found in any other primary source.

Emily's journal is invaluable in settling innumerable dates, but it often poses more questions than it solves. Whether the original was more accurate, or to what extent, is unknown; it was unfortunately destroyed. In its present form it often contains several days' events or observations under one date; once or twice two months are shown as one. Evidence from other sources may provide the required confirmation. It is clear, for example, that the Duke and Duchess of Argyll accepted Tennyson's suggestion of 5 April 1860 to visit the Isle of Wight and see him at Farringford, despite the whooping-cough that had afflicted his family, though the record of their 'three evenings with him' is given under March in Emily's journal.

Too often, therefore, we find ourselves in the margin of conjecture, knowing that a given date may be only probable or approximate, knowing also that the incidence of such imprecisions may not always be suspected. As if to sound a warning note, this recurring uncertainty begins with the date of Tennyson's birth.

If the chronological method of presenting a writer's life has the advantage over the biographical of greater regard for continuity and precision (the biographer being able to take evasive action when confronted with dating uncertainties), its author has less scope for character assessment, or for background settings, and little for enlarging on aspects of his subject's work or topics of significant interest at various stages of his life. On the other hand he has little opportunity to fall into the common biographical error of allowing bias or prejudice to slant or fictionalize his work. The whole evidence suggests, for example, that, whatever resentments or irritation may have temporarily marred two of their excursions, Tennyson prized Palgrave's friendship, and his individual judgment, more highly than recent biography tends to allow. Authorial prejudice may be found in the selection of contemporary impressions, but wherever bias is implicit in a chronology it is far more likely to be the contemporary observer's; Carlyle's condemnation in November 1873 of one whose genius he admired reflects his own character at least as much as Tennyson's. To see Tennyson as his contemporaries saw him is one of the more incidental aims of this work; another is to provide glimpses of settings, and to sample, whenever appropriate, observations in Emily's journal which have a vividness of poetic touch reminiscent of Dorothy Wordsworth's.

Illustrations of Tennyson's activities, apart from his writing, must be limited and incidental. It is impossible to convey how much he read or translated aloud for Emily's benefit as she relaxed, or how much he read for his own pleasure or instruction in his 'den' or his study; he was an avid reader of novels, and few major works of the age, whatever the subject, escaped his attention. It is astonishing that one so visually handicapped that more than once he thought he was going blind could have remained a compulsive reader most of his life. Similarly one can do little to indicate the time he devoted to Hallam and Lionel from childhood onwards, in games and education, on local walks and during long holidays. Only readers familiar with Emily's journal can realize how much time he and his family spent in gardening and working in the fields on their Farringford estate. Entertaining guests at Farringford and Aldworth, and meeting friends in London, occupied an enormous amount of his time over many years.

With such a variety of domestic, rural, social, and metropolitan engagements, Tennyson's time for writing was limited. Such was the technical virtuosity he had achieved after composing abundantly in his early years, and so much time did he habitually spend in incidental unwritten composition, that the actual penning of his poetry in his adult years probably occupied but a small proportion of his life; he may have spent almost as much in reading his poetry aloud and revising it before agreeing to have it published. Nor was the later Tennyson often driven to write poetry. Not until he became interested in historical drama did he find extensive subjects which absorbed him from start to finish. *In Memoriam* and *Idylls of the King* grew over long periods, and it was not until their later stages that he conceived them as entities, and expanded them to give unity of design (more successfully with the former than with the latter). But for subjects, usually narrative, suggested by friends, mainly at Emily's invitation, and a Laureate sense of duty which made him respond to State occasions such as the burial of the Duke of Wellington, imperial or international exhibitions, and royal celebrations or mourning, there was little to hold Tennyson's poetic thinking long except those abiding metaphysical questions which stemmed from the staunchness of his faith during an age of transition. Like Arthur Hallam and his own brother Charles Turner, he believed that religion and the expanding truth of science must be compatible; but nothing could alter his conviction that Jesus was both human and divine, and that the human soul is immortal. The thought that there could be no life after death made him distraught and irrationally Pauline; Positivism or 'the religion of Humanity' was an aversion to him.

The majority of Victorian readers turned to Tennyson's poetry for spiritual assurance and comfort. Queen Victoria herself did, and one wonders whether the royal links with the Poet Laureate would have continued to strengthen as they did had she not lost her husband, the Prince Consort, so early; whether, too, Tennyson would have been such a public figure, sought out and befriended by aristocrats and imperial administrators, had not this royal recognition been intimate and lasting. T. S. Eliot argued that he was 'the surface flatterer of his own time' and 'the most perfect conformist'; it would be nearer the truth, though still misleading, to say that he was a bundle of contradictions. Apart from the intellectuals with whom he found kinship in the main areas of research and discovery, he belonged in various ways to two different worlds, satiety with one impelling him to seek relief in the other. He was the poetic recluse of Mablethorpe or Farringford who needed to meet old friends or upper-class society in London. To escape unwelcome visitors who ruined his seclusion at Farringford he planned to have a remote cottage on Blackdown; this became Aldworth, a mansion which was both a retreat and a place fit to entertain the many celebrities he numbered among his friends. His brother Frederick believed it was Emily Tennyson who was ambitious; if so, it was for the sake of her sons, and neither parent neglected opportunities for promoting their future.

Both were conscious of national injustices, and it is probable that, as their own advantages increased, the need for social and economic reforms preyed more and more on their minds. Not long after Gladstone became prime minister in 1868, Emily suggested to him a utopian scheme of taxation and administration for the general good; soon after becoming a peer, and seeking a d'Eyncourt title, Tennyson advocated a further extension of the franchise. One of the articles of his creed, he informed Gladstone, was 'The nation is one and includes all ranks of people.' He had long felt deeply on such issues, though as a poet he thought it prudent to quicken his readers' sense of wrong ventriloquially, in dramatic lyrical works such as *Maud* and his 'Locksley Hall' poems. Influenced by Carlyle, F. D. Maurice, and Kingsley, conscience and integrity made him voice his protest against abuses and deprivation. The fanciful elaboration of *The Princess* is motivated by a passionate plea for women's full rights in education and the partnership of marriage. Whatever the divergent tendencies of his life (manifestations of his individual genius and its need for recognition), in one thing at least he was consistent: he was a true patriot, critical, anxious for the well-being of the country and its empire, and seemingly somewhat disillusioned and pessimistic near the end.

After referring to his father's concern for the welfare of the British Empire and his interest in proposed old-age pension schemes, Hallam wrote in the last chapter of his memoir:

> The mere working on behalf of party, as far as his own conviction went, was to him unintelligible, as well as the love of power and of rule for their own sakes. That all should work conscientiously and harmoniously together for the common weal, each with such differing power as had been given to each man, recognising the value of the difference, was his highest ideal of government.

For the expression of his finer and more elevated thoughts in general, Tennyson turned to poetry. The Chronology helps to place much of this in perspective, and is particularly helpful on the final shaping of *The Princess* and the evolution of *Idylls of the King*.

A Tennyson Chronology

Ancestry, and Early Years (1809–26)

The Tennysons, thought to be of Danish origin, seem to have settled first in Holderness, the region east of Hull. Their descendants belonged mainly to small yeomen and professional classes. Michael T, an apothecary at Hedon, married the heiress of the wealthy Clayton family who owned most of Grimsby before its development, and claimed descent from holders of the d'Eyncourt baronetcy. Their son George (1750–1835), the poet's grandfather, became a solicitor (like his grandfather), set up practice at Market Rasen in Lincolnshire, and married Mary Turner of Caistor, a gentle, devoted, devout, and artistically inclined young woman. George inherited his father's wealth and property, and showed and transmitted some of the Clayton hotheadedness and temperamental instability. He was a shrewd business man, learning much as a legal consultant on land enclosures, and acquiring land on favourable terms whenever he had the opportunity.

In this way he became the owner of Beacons, once d'Eyncourt property, with traces of an old castle, on the edge of the Lincolnshire Wolds at Tealby, three miles from Market Rasen. Plans for its improvement were soon under way, and the Tennysons occupied it about 1801, after attempting to raise their social status (unsuccessfully) at Deloraine Court in Lincoln, then living for a while at Grimsby. The new home was called Tealby Lodge; about 1811, in furtherance of d'Eyncourt pretensions, it was renamed Bayons Manor.

George and Mary T had four children: Elizabeth, Mary, George Clayton (the poet's father, b. 1778), and Charles (b. 1784). Elizabeth, beautiful and charming, married the heir of a rich Durham coalfield-owner, and lived at Brancepeth Castle. Purchased by her father-in-law, this had been converted into a splendid residence, extravagant improvements to which in medieval style her brother Charles was to emulate at Bayons Manor. Her husband enjoyed considerable political power from the acquisition of pocket boroughs. Mary, the younger sister, became Calvinistic, and married a local Nonconformist squire, John Bourne of Dalby. The two sons were sent to St Peter's Grammar School, York, and, after private tutoring for George in Huntingdonshire and a period at Louth Grammar School for Charles, to St John's College, Cambridge.

Very tall and strong, George Clayton T suffered in youth from physical awkwardness and instability; in him were combined his father's intractable nature and his mother's sweetness. He was subject to moodiness, melancholy, and outbreaks of ungovernable temper; the epilepsy from which he was to suffer was already apparent. He had considerable gifts and could have done well at Cambridge, but told his father that academic success demanded too much exertion, and finished with a poor pass degree.

As Charles offered every prospect of being sensible, efficient, and amenable, his father had little doubt, even when his boys were young, that he would have to make him his heir and deny George the rights of primogeniture. He always intended, however, to ensure that the latter, and his family, would have an adequate inheritance. George found himself destined for the Church against his will. After being ordained in 1801, he was allowed (as if in compensation, though he probably did not know his father's intentions at the time) to visit Russia, from which he returned with exciting (sometimes improbable) stories, after a prolonged absence.

He was ordained priest in December 1802, becoming rector of Benniworth (a living worth about £500 p.a.), with duties also at South Willingham (both parishes near Market Rasen). Later he took lodgings at Louth, where he became engaged to Elizabeth Fytche, daughter of a previous vicar. They were married in 1805, with expectations, which they realized in 1806, of additional income from the livings of Somersby and Bag Enderby, two small parishes in beautiful wold country east of Horncastle. Delayed by alterations and extensions, they did not occupy the new rectory, formerly the manor house, until early in 1808.

Twelve children were born to them, ten at Somersby: George, born at Bayons Manor (he died only a few weeks old in 1806); Frederick, born at Louth in 1807; Charles, born in 1808; Alfred, 1809; Mary, 1810; Emily, 1811; Edward, 1813; Arthur, 1814; Septimus, 1815; Matilda, 1816; Cecilia, 1817; Horatio, 1819. At one time Tennyson used to say he was born on 5 August 1809; according to H. D. Rawnsley, the Somersby baptismal register gives the 5th. The poet's son Hallam thought that the register seemed to confirm that date, but placed more reliance on T's statement that his mother always kept his birthday on the 6th, 'and I suppose she knew'. (It was the fourth anniversary of her wedding.)

In 1815, two years after purchasing the degree of Doctor of Civil Law, George T received a considerable increase in his income when his father procured him an additional living, at Grimsby. He could now afford a carriage and pair. He was happiest away from his crowded home. As a magistrate he was always welcome, for his geniality and brilliant conversation, at the barristers' mess during Sessions at Spilsby. Not far off, at Halton Holgate, lived his best friend, the Revd T. H. Rawnsley.

Dr T played the harp, and was genuinely interested in the arts and architecture. In 1820, partly in order to entertain his visitors, he built a Gothic dining-room with the help of his coachman, carving the oak chimney-piece himself to make it look like stone. He was a great reader; his library included Greek and Latin as well as English literature, volumes on theology, history, philosophy, science, and travel, and a large number of books, including valuable folio editions, bought at a local sale, when possessions of the deceased Bennet Langton, Samuel Johnson's friend and successor as Professor of Ancient Literature at the Royal Academy, were auctioned.

Dr Tennyson, a most exacting scholar, taught his three eldest boys Greek and Latin before they were sent to Louth Grammar School; Alfred could recite Horace's odes before he joined his elder brothers there at the age seven. Frederick, the eldest and most brilliant, was transferred to Eton in 1818; Alfred was withdrawn from Louth in 1820 because he was unhappy at an institution where discipline was frighteningly enforced, and boys were often brutally violent. Even here both he and Charles earned reputations for their skill in writing verse.

Their mother had made a practice of reading poetry to them, and Alfred was about eight when he proved himself to Charles by writing Thomsonian lines in praise of flowers. Reading aloud fostered his love of fine-sounding words and phrases. Pope's translation of Homer's *Iliad* was his favourite work some two or three years later, when he wrote hundreds of lines in 'the regular Popeian metre'. At one time he claimed to have written 'an epic poem of great length' in the *Marmion* style when he was ten; this must have been the 'epic of six thousand lines à la Walter Scott' which he informed his son Hallam had been composed 'about twelve and onward', chiefly on battles, and sea and mountain scenery. He used to write about seventy lines at a time, and go 'shouting them about the fields in the dark'. Such was his enthusiasm for Byron that, on hearing of his death in April 1824, 'the whole world seemed to be darkened', and he carved the words 'Byron is dead' on a rock in Holywell glen. (The lure of Keats and Shelley came later.)

His father also was a poet, and probably encouraged his verse translations from classical authors, a few remarkable examples of which survive from the 1820–3 period. More astonishing is *The Devil and the Lady*, a lively, informed drama in blank verse which T claimed to have written at the age of fourteen; a fragment, set in Spain, survives from another play he wrote about the same time. Other pieces, written at the age of fourteen to fifteen, are 'The Bridal' (after reading Scott's *The Bride of Lammermoor*) and 'The Coach of Death' (one of those precocious successes his fellow-students loved to hear him read at Cambridge). Episodes in the campaigns of Wellington and Napoleon afforded other subjects for the early poetic talents of both Charles and Alfred.

At home the children played on the lawn between the rectory and its gardens, or about Baumber's Farm, a red-brick neighbouring house with a battlemented parapet. The reading of Malory's *Morte d'Arthur* led to jousting in mock tournaments, and, for Alfred, an idealization of King Arthur that lasted all his life. The elder boys fished in the brook, or wandered about the southern wolds. Brothers and sisters composed serial stories collectively for reading after dinner. For their holidays they travelled across 'the drain-cut levels of the marshy lea' to the coast at Mablethorpe; sometimes to Skegness. They visited their paternal grandparents, or their aunt Mary at Dalby. Alfred remembered her weeping to think that by God's mercy she was one of the Elect, though no better than her neighbours; once she told him that the sight of him reminded her of the Scriptural words 'Depart from me, ye cursed, into everlasting fire'.

In a letter to W. F. Rawnsley on 2 April 1889, Tennyson writes: 'Young Hyde, the saddler in Louth, gave me one of his strong cigars when I was a boy of fourteen, and I smoked it all, and flung the end into a horsepond, and I was none the worse; so I was bound to be a smoker.' (He could never break the habit, and so heavily did he smoke at certain periods, particularly before his marriage, that the addiction, coupled with the drinking of strong port, made him a ruminant poet, many of whose compositions were lost in mental clouds.)

The sense of injustice which was fostered in Dr Tennyson by his relatively restricted circumstances and aversion to parish work was fuelled by thoughts of his brother's success in politics, and of the social opportunities he enjoyed in London, at Bayons Manor, and at Brancepeth Castle. His gloomy resentment led to angry outbreaks, so insufferable at times that Alfred would go out into the darkness, throw himself on a grave in the churchyard, and pray for burial beneath the sod. The rector's health suffered, and in 1822 he and his wife stayed at Cheltenham, hoping the waters would effect a cure. His improvement was short-lived; he could not refrain from bouts of alcoholism, and his seizures became more frequent and alarming.

Charles had been at home since 1821, and he and Alfred were taught by their father, whose extravagances continued. He now employed a valet, a coachman, a supervisory housekeeper, a cook, and a governess, besides housemaids and gardeners. In 1824 he complained that as many as twenty-three people had to sleep in the house. His father ('the Old Man of the Wolds', as he was known to the Somersby family) had increased his annual allowance to £700, paid off outstanding debts, and agreed to pay £60 p.a. for the education of each of the younger sons at Louth or any similar school (excluding Eton, which had done little to improve Frederick, his accent especially).

1825 Alfred seems to be on good terms with his relatives, and not averse to visiting them.

(2 Aug) He writes to his uncle Charles on his father's continued attacks, two since his grandfather's visit of little more than a week ago.

(20 Aug) His grandmother dies at Bayons Manor. Soon afterwards he writes a poem on the subject, at the request of his grandfather, who rewards him with half a guinea, 'the first you have ever earned by poetry, and take my word for it, the last'.

(8 Oct) He returns to Somersby on foot after spending the

night at Louth because of a threatening storm while he was on his way from Bayons Manor.

(9 Oct) He sets off early to Dalby, where he writes to his grandfather. His uncle and aunt are at the seaside, but he proposes to stay until they are back in a day or two.

(30 Oct) His uncle Charles having promised to show them to the poet Thomas Moore, T sends him a further instalment of his poems.

1826 Early this year his father begins a regular recourse to laudanum (probably prescribed in the first place) for his chest pains, and this and other drugs, including soporifics, combined with alcoholic excesses, worsen his condition. Such is the neglect of home and family, and the strain caused by his alarming outbreaks and intemperate language, that Alfred, who had been sustained by family affection and loyalty, especially for his mother (whose example he admired; cf. the poem 'Isabel'), and for his brother Charles, begins to fail in health, so much so by the early summer that Frederick, who has left Eton, requests his grandfather to send money so that he can take his brother to Mablethorpe for a 'sea-bathing'cure. Dr T's health and behaviour continue to worsen; Mrs T is frightened, and the traumatic effect on Alfred and his elder brothers remains deep for much of their lives. At the time Alfred can still take refuge in poetry. In addition to 'Armageddon' he has scores of shorter pieces, many of them inspired by striking passages in his father's books.

1827

Early in the year Charles and Alfred send a proposal for the publication of *Poems by Two Brothers* to J. and J. Jackson, booksellers at Louth. (A few of Frederick's poems are included.)

9 February Charles and Alfred acknowledge the receipt of £20, the sum agreed for the copyright of the volume. Some of it has to be expended in books from Jacksons'.)

Returning a batch of proof-sheets some time later, they send a preface and an introductory poem, the last six lines of which are subsequently replaced by ten. They do not wish the initials

C. and A. T. (which the publishers had appended) to appear at the end of the preface.

March About this time the Old Man of the Wolds increases Dr T's annual grant to £1000, making allowance for Frederick's expenses at Cambridge.

20 April *Poems by Two Brothers* is published anonymously. (Years later Charles said that he and Alfred celebrated the day by driving in a hired carriage to Mablethorpe, where they 'shared their triumph with the winds and waves' by reciting their verses at the top of their voices until they were hoarse.)

4 June Aunt Elizabeth informs their grandfather that Charles and Alfred (in London with their mother) have called on her in Berkeley Square. Alfred's second call reveals that the only thing which had 'particularly charmed' him was Westminster Abbey. She wishes he had other interests besides his poetry, which is 'beautiful'.

Summer The rector becomes more violent, and Mrs T tries unsuccessfully to get her children away.

October Charles enters Trinity College, Cambridge, with Frederick, transferred from St John's and already distinguished by winning the Browne Medal for a Greek ode. At the end of the month Alfred is staying with his grandfather at Bayons Manor. His aim is to obtain tuition in mathematics (the cost of which Aunt Elizabeth is to pay) to prepare for admission to Cambridge next year.

November Early this month Dr Tennyson agrees to visit France with his brother Charles, who promises first to bring him to Bayons Manor. Not wishing to meet him, and unable to find a congenial tutor, Alfred suddenly decides to set out for Cambridge, where he arrives on the evening of the 9th. After examination by the Dean and Dr Whewell (who is to be his tutor in mathematics and moral philosophy), he is accepted at Trinity. (Before entering the University he had studied history and natural science, read his classics, and written Latin and Greek odes plus a Homeric book in Greek hexameters on the Seven against Thebes.) At dinner in hall he is noticed by W. H. Thompson, later Master of Trinity, who thinks, 'That man must be a poet.'

15 (Thurs) Dr T leaves Bayons Manor with his brother for London.

23 Grandfather George informs his daughter Elizabeth what provisions he is making for the Somersby family, and refers to the £100 she has promised for Alfred's maintenance at Cambridge.

30 Alfred's father writes to him from Paris, expressing a wish to hear from him.

December On the 5th Alfred writes to his father. At the end of the term he and Charles move from Rose Crescent, where they have shared rooms with Frederick, to 57 Corpus Buildings, Trumpington Street. They are back at Somersby by the 10th.

1828

January Alfred and Charles have been staying 'some time' with their grandmother at Louth by the 15th. On the 20th Dr T reaches England. His three sons have left for Cambridge before he returns to Somersby.

3 April Back at Somersby, Alfred informs his grandfather that Dr T cannot accept the invitation to Bayons Manor, as their cook is dying, after setting fire to her dress.

18 April From Cambridge T writes to his aunt Elizabeth (who continues to send him £100 p.a. until after his marriage), complaining about the dullness of the level countryside, the monotony of student revelry, and boredom from University studies, mathematics in particular. A few days earlier he had been at Dalby with his aunt Mary. He has been trying to obtain a copy of *Falkland* (Bulwer-Lytton's first novel, 1827, passages of which were to influence some of his poems, including 'Mariana').

Summer The first three parts of 'The Lover's Tale' may have been completed at this stage, if not earlier.

October At the beginning of the new academic year George Hildeyard T, Charles's son, enters Trinity; his cousins help him to find lodgings. Arthur Hallam, son of the historian Henry Hallam, and the Etonian friend of Gladstone, is another new entrant; he has spent several months in Italy.

December Frederick T is rusticated for three terms, for not attending chapel and for being impertinent to the governing body when asked to explain.

1829

26 January (Mon) Grandfather George complains to his son Charles about the behaviour of Charles and Alfred (who left him on Friday), and the manner in which they and Frederick are wasting half their father's income; they are much worse 'since they went to Cambridge'.

4 February Dr T informs his father that Alfred and Charles are misled by Frederick, who has no respect for authority at home; he regrets sending him to Eton.

20 February He has Frederick evicted. (F stays three days with Mr Baumber, the constable who took charge of him, then with his aunt at Louth.)

March The rector is so violent and threatening, the family leave him at Somersby. Mrs T goes to Louth. T. H. Rawnsley takes care of Dr T at Halton Holgate, and is convinced he must not be allowed to return to his family.

To please his father, Alfred decides with considerable reluctance (probably during the Easter vacation) to submit a poem for the Chancellor's Gold Medal, the set subject being Timbuctoo. (Just when T worked on it is not clear. About half was taken from 'Armageddon'; to this was added a beginning and an end, the whole leading up to the Keatsian theme of the idealizing Imagination which is threatened by Discovery or scientific truth – a conflict quite foreign to T's later poetic beliefs.)

14 May Dr T leaves for Paris.

During the summer term at Cambridge friendship between T and Arthur Hallam grows. AH admires T's poems; T is fascinated by Hallam's precocious brilliance, his rhetorical skill (verse included), his wide-ranging knowledge, and, above all perhaps, his search for a religion from which no truth is excluded. (The despondency which sometimes afflicted AH finds relief in their shared idealism, sometimes in the mimicry with which T regaled his friends. 'The Two Voices' may include some of their opposing arguments, for AH, often ill and subject to painful headaches, entertained suicidal thoughts.)

6 June T is announced winner of the Chancellor's Medal; he thinks AH should have won it.

29 June T invites his friend Charles Merivale (last year's Medal winner) to read his poem at Commencement (the day when degrees are conferred on 'commencing' bachelors).

5 July Merivale reads T's 'Timbuctoo' in the Senate House. (T couldn't face the public recitation, he admitted in his old age.)

12 July He sends his grandfather two copies of the prize-winning poem, and gives 'indisposition' (with a reference to treatment by an eye-specialist in London) as the reason for not reciting it himself.

In the absence of their father (now a traveller in Switzerland, later in Italy), the younger Tennysons enjoy their summer at Somersby, giving parties and visiting friends, including the Rawnsleys. In this way they probably become acquainted with the Sellwood sisters from Horncastle, who often stayed at Harrington Hall with their cousins, the Cracrofts. T, who had thought of publishing again with Charles, has agreed with AH on a joint publication of poems.

31 October T becomes one of the Apostles, an exclusive group which began as the Cambridge Conversazione Society at St John's College. (As, in time, its leading members came from Trinity, its meetings were held there. Membership being restricted to twelve, they became known facetiously as 'The Apostles', a title to which they had no objection. In the early prime of the group, John Sterling was its most brilliant figure and F. D. Maurice its spiritual leader. They met on Saturday evenings, usually in the room of the reader of the paper for discussion, subjects ranging from science, literature, and philosophy, to theology and politics.)

November Notes on three of the four meetings or 'Acts' of the Apostles:
7 Tennyson pays five shillings for non-attendance.
21 To the question whether Shelley's poems have an immoral tendency, T and AH vote *no*.
28 To the question whether there is any rule of moral action except general expediency, they vote *aye*.

5 December At the last meeting of the Apostles for the Michaelmas term AH reads his paper on whether the existence of an intelligent First Cause is deducible from the phenomena of the universe. To this question he and T vote *no*.

(The three Tennysons have contributed to an enthusiasm for Shelley's poetry at Cambridge, where a group of students have published 500 copies of 'Adonais' from a printed text said to have been brought from Italy by AH. The other poets in vogue are Wordsworth, Coleridge, and Keats; Byron is on the wane.

Affairs at Somersby had undoubtedly helped to induce a lotos-eater complex in T, and hero-worship of him as a poet at Cambridge, where some incline to think him the equal of Milton, tends to keep him happily circumscribed.

Next to AH, James Spedding is the closest of T's friends, a group which includes John Kemble, Richard Monckton Milnes, William Brookfield, W. H. Thompson, Robert Monteith, and J. W. Blakesley.)

AH takes Charles and Alfred T to London at the end of term, and introduces them to some of his Eton friends; they see Fanny Kemble, John's sister, in her first play. After returning to Cambridge to hear a debate on Milton at the Union, they travel to Somersby, where AH stays a few days before Christmas, and is exceedingly happy in the kind of family companionship he had never previously known; in retrospect he thought he fell in love with T's sister Emily almost at first sight.

1830

January Before returning to Cambridge, T probably busies himself revising poems for publication.

13 February T is unable to read his expected paper (on ghosts) at the Apostles' meeting, and resigns his seat.

14 March Charles T's *Sonnets and Fugitive Pieces* is published at Cambridge.

April Hallam, at Somersby partly to consider and prepare for his joint publication with T, makes known his love for Emily. One day the Sellwoods drive over from Horncastle; AH asks Emily Sellwood to walk with him in Holywell glen, where T, coming upon them suddenly, archly asks whether she is a dryad or an oread (a meeting Emily remembers for the rest of her life). T finishes copying up the poems he intends for publication, but loses the whole manuscript when walking home one night from Spilsby. (How much he had to rely on memory for preparing a new copy is not clear.)

May At Cambridge T has learned that AH has acceded to his father's advice not to publish his poems.

June T's *Poems, Chiefly Lyrical* is published by Effingham Wilson in London, AH having acted as an intermediary. At the end of the month Dr T returns to England.

5 July T, very ill according to his mother, has gone to London to consult an eminent physician (he has been staying with the Hallams at 67 Wimpole Street, and has already left for the Spanish frontier). Frederick has also left Somersby.

July (end) Their father returns to his rectory, with hair-raising stories of his Continental adventures.

(John Sterling had become very friendly with General Torrijos, leader of Spanish Constitutionalist exiles in London, and his cousin Robert Boyd had bought a ship to transport them to Spain. The ship was seized when the Spanish Government protested. Sterling crossed the Channel in an open boat with Torrijos, who met Boyd in Gibraltar, where the conspirators gathered. Members of the Apostles had volunteered their help in what seemed to them a liberating cause. John Kemble and R. C. Trench helped Boyd at Gibraltar. AH and T set out on 2 July to meet northern confederates in the Pyrenees, taking an indirect route via Paris, Poitiers, and the Mediterranean coast. Afterwards they relaxed at Cauteretz, around which they saw mountain scenery which made an indelible impression on T, inspiring images in 'Oenone', part of which he wrote at the time, and in later poems.)

September

8 (Wed) They begin their return from Bordeaux, on the steamer *Leeds*, bound for Dublin. (Trench and Kemble stay at Gibraltar until early 1831. In November the Governor orders the Constitutionalists to leave. Accompanied by Boyd, they slip out in two vessels, only to be captured and executed on the beach near Malaga.)

12 T and AH are in Dublin, after a rough voyage.

20 They take the first train to run between Liverpool and Manchester. (The statesman William Huskisson is fatally injured when it starts, and T, who has not been able to see the rails, because of crowding spectators, his myopia, and the darkness, imagines the wheels moving in grooves; cf. 'Locksley Hall', 182.)

October Both feeling unwell, probably as a result of their father's presence at home, Charles and Alfred delay their departure for Cambridge two weeks.

2 November They return to college. (According to Blakesley, Alfred looks better than ever in a fortnight.)

3 November AH sends a transcription of T's 'Anacaona' to W. B. Donne, an Apostle who had, for religious reasons, left Cambridge without graduating.

December (early) Reform agitators are responsible for riots in the country outside Cambridge, and a threat is made to attack the town and burn down the University library. Undergraduates, including the Apostles, arm themselves with sticks to help the constabulary, but no attack is made. T and other students help to save a farmhouse at Coton after arsonists have started a blaze.

December (later) The poet Wordsworth has been staying with his brother Christopher, Master of Trinity, and is aware of the poetic promise shown by Charles and Alfred T. On the evening of the 19th he is entertained by James Spedding, winner of the Declamation Prize, and son of his old school friend. Several students (not including the Ts and AH, who have gone to Somersby) meet to hear him; unforgetful of mob violence and excesses in Paris, and alarmed by events in Europe and political agitation at home, he chooses to talk on revolutions. After a brief visit to Somersby, probably to seek Dr T's approval of his virtual engagement to Emily, AH proceeds to London for Christmas. (Each is nineteen.)

1831

January *Poems, Chiefly Lyrical* (already favourably reviewed in August) is commended anonymously by W. J. Fox in *The Westminster Review.*

13 February AH sends Donne a copy of T's early version of 'Mariana in the South', set in barren country he and Alfred had seen in Mediterranean France.

February (late) Merivale's impression is that T 'is trying to make his eyes bad enough for an aegrotat degree'. Charles and Alfred are called home because their father is dying; T is not expected to return. They give a supper in their rooms before departing, and Alfred's last sight in Trumpington Street is 'Thompson's handsome face under the light of a street lamp'. An agreement has been reached between Dr T and Henry Hallam that AH shall not visit Somersby until he reaches his majority (i.e. for more than a year).

March

3 (Thurs) Leigh Hunt's favourable review of Charles and Alfred T's poems is concluded in *The Tatler*. (It began on 24 Feb, and was written in response to an appeal by AH.)

16 Dr T dies peacefully.

24 He is buried at Somersby, six neighbouring clergymen acting as pall-bearers; (Mrs T had wished him to be buried at Tealby, but his father had raised objections). Of the Old Man of the Wolds' family, only Mrs Bourne attends; Charles is represented by his son George Hildeyard T. That night Alfred sleeps in his father's bed, hoping to see his ghost.

(Mrs T has more than an adequate income; of this her father-in-law provides £800 p.a. He pays off the family debts, including £650 accumulated at Cambridge by her three sons. As the rectory is not required until the patron Mr Burton can install his son as rector, the Ts stay on at Somersby.)

4 April Alfred and Charles are expected to dine with the Revd T. H. Rawnsley at Halton Holgate. He has urged them and Frederick to make full use of their talents 'for their own maintenance and Respectability'.

April (later) and early May T is distressed about his eyes, and afraid he will lose his sight. His uncle Charles thinks he has persuaded him to enter the Church.

August AH's anonymous and laudatory review of *Poems, Chiefly Lyrical* appears in *The Englishman's Magazine* (a short-lived periodical just taken over by Edward Moxon), together with the sonnet 'Check every outflash', which he has sent without T's permission. On the 14th AH asks Merivale to call on Moxon to see how much he would pay T for monthly contributions to his magazine; T no longer intends entering the Church.

September (early) T accompanies his sister Emily to Cheltenham for treatment of recurrent pain in her side (they are still there on the 19th).

October AH visits them early in the month, leaving T in 'precarious health'. T's 'Anacreontics', 'No More' (written when he was seventeen), and 'A Fragment' appear in *The Gem* for 1831.

2 December Charles T informs his friend John Hookham Frere that T has just been on a visit to Cambridge.

16 December T is there again to hear AH deliver his prize declamation in Trinity Chapel; Hallam has also won the college English essay prize.

1832

January AH and Charles and Frederick T graduate at Cambridge.

26 February AH is at Cambridge, on his way to Somersby, where he stays during the whole of March. (He came of age on 1 Feb.)

18 March At Somersby T acknowledges the £100 he has received from his aunt Elizabeth Russell, and says his 'blindness increases daily'.

18 April It is the Easter vacation. Brookfield and R. J. Tennant have been staying with the Ts at Somersby, and Robert Monteith and his friend Francis Garden are expected (on their way to Cambridge).

21 April Writing to Emily, AH asks her to copy the concluding stanzas of 'The Miller's Daughter' for him. He has heard from her that T had gone to Sutton-on-Sea, near Mablethorpe.

May The poem most read and discussed by Apostolic friends at Cambridge is T's 'The Palace of Art', the outcome of Trench's memorable remark, 'Tennyson, we cannot live in art.' A review of *Poems, Chiefly Lyrical* by 'Christopher North' appears in *Blackwood's Magazine*. In it Professor John Wilson, provoked by the reviews of Fox and Hallam (especially the latter's eulogy of the 'Cockney school' of poetry), makes fun of T's weaker poems, but praises and illustrates his 'fine faculties'.

June

At Cambridge with his friend Tennant early this month, T talks of 'going abroad instantly'.

14 (Thurs) AH informs Kemble that T may reach London 'today'. (During this visit T stays for a while with John Kemble. Old friends assemble and discuss 'The Palace of Art' and 'A Dream of Fair Women'. T discusses his next volume

of poetry with AH, rambles with him in London, and smokes with him in his 'den' at the top of 67 Wimpole Street.)

21 Alfred is in Southampton Row, 'smoking all the day', Spedding reports. AH and T attend *The Hunchback*, starring Fanny Kemble at Covent Garden Theatre.

22 T goes to Richmond 'intending to write an Innkeeper's Daughter' (lost, if ever written) at the Star and Garter, and complaining about his illness and incompatibility with Frederick. He dines with the Hallams in Wimpole Street, and is very nervous.

31 He and AH set off for a Rhineland tour.

July (early) Because of a cholera epidemic they are quarantined for the first week in a vessel near a muddy island in the Maas river, where T is 'bugbitten, flybitten, fleabitten, gnatbitten, and hungerbitten'. Eventually they become so annoyed by the delay that they pull down the Dutch colours on the steamboat, and reverse them. They are then allowed to stay in Rotterdam.

11 July They resume their journey slowly up the Rhine.

16 July Now at Nonnenwerth, they have visited Cologne (T is in raptures with the cathedral) and Bonn, and climbed the Drachenfels.

August

5–6 (Sun–Mon) At Trinity, Cambridge, on their way to Somersby, and 'fresh from the Rhine' (they had sailed as far as Bingen, returning via Aix-la-Chapelle [Aachen] and Brussels), they meet Spedding.

c.12–22 At Somersby AH learns that Frederick T has quarrelled with his grandfather over what seems to be his disinheritance. On the 21st, wishing to have his marriage allowance settled, Hallam visits T. H. Rawnsley, who, as Emily's guardian, is in correspondence with his father.

25 Henry Hallam informs Rawnsley that he cannot allow his son more than £600 a year.

September (late) T sends AH copies of many poems for Moxon to publish, including 'To J. S.', lines written for James Spedding after the loss of his brother Edward on 24 August, and 'To Christopher

North', a 'silly squib' ill-advisedly printed to make his reviewer squirm. AH acknowledges receipt of the poems on the 24th.

10 October AH at Croydon has taken time off from his legal studies to read proofs of T's poems with Douglas Heath and W. H. Thompson. He informs T that Moxon is anxious to have the remainder of his manuscripts.

13 October T returns proofs to Moxon; he is not in a hurry to publish, and has not yet decided how much to include in the volume.

20 November Although the first two parts are already in print, T has resolved not to have 'The Lover's Tale' published; 'it is too full of faults'. AH protests in vain.

December
5 (Wed) *Poems* (dated 1833) is already out; nearly a hundred copies have been sold in two days.
8 *The Literary Gazette* is harshly critical of T's new volume.
23 AH comes to Somersby for Christmas and the New Year (Emily is ill).

1833

January W. J. Fox has some good things to say of T's *Poems* in *The Monthly Repository,* placing him second to Wordsworth and Coleridge among living poets. Edward Bulwer (later Bulwer-Lytton) attacks T's poetry anonymously in *The New Monthly Magazine*; he associates T with Keats and Shelley in 'the Cockney School', and charges him with effeminacy and affectation.

February A letter late in the month from AH to Emily suggests that T has been reading books he sent her in January, including Jane Austen's *Emma*. (Hallam's continued reading of Jane Austen may have stimulated T to further reading of this author.)

March Early in the month T is at Mablethorpe. Late in the month he is in London with his sister Mary ('with the professed purpose of studying the Elgin marbles', Blakesley hears).

April

4 (Thurs) They visit the Zoological Gardens with AH.

5 All three examine through a huge microscope 'the lions and tigers which lie perdus in a drop of spring water'.

6 They visit the Tower of London.

7 They all hear 'a magnificent Handel anthem' in Westminster Abbey.

8 AH's mother and sister take Mary, 'a decided favorite' with all, to Kensington Gardens, Hyde Park, and the Pantechnicon in Belgrave Square.

9 After another visit to the Gallery of Practical Science, T stays late into the night at Moxon's, where he enjoys Leigh Hunt's company and compliments.

10 The Ts stay at Cambridge on their way home.

At Somersby T is crushed by the heavy sarcasm with which John Wilson Croker has treated his *Poems* in *The Quarterly Review*, 'To Christopher North' and 'O Darling Room' especially. AH is ill during the second half of the month.

June After a period at Mablethorpe, T stays a week at Cambridge before going to London with Frederick T, Monteith, and Stephen Spring Rice.

July He leaves London for Scotland, where he spends the later part of the month, most of it with Monteith at his home near Carstairs.

3 August AH, after visiting Emily at Somersby, leaves with his father for Vienna. (It seems very unlikely that T left Scotland to see him before his departure; if so, it could not have been in response to the letter AH wrote late on 31 July. The supper with Tennant, Moxon, and Leigh Hunt, at which T recited fragments of 'The Gardener's Daughter', and their visit to Samuel Rogers' gallery of paintings and library, where T was chagrined to find his brother's volume of poetry but not his own, could have taken place in June–July.)

October (early) A letter addressed to T, written by Henry Elton (AH's uncle) at Clifton on 1 October, and reporting AH's death of apoplexy in Vienna on 15 September (the autopsy revealed brain-haemorrhage), is brought home by Matilda T from

Spilsby, where she has had her dancing-lesson. John Heath, T's Cambridge friend, is present (he seems to have fallen in love with Mary T in London).

10 October Writing from Clifton, Henry Hallam requests T to meet him next Thursday (the 17th) at 67 Wimpole Street, and sends assurance of his 'heart-felt and lasting affection' to Emily.

25 October Edward FitzGerald has heard that T has been in London 'for some time; he has been making fresh poems, which are finer, they say, than any he has done'; they include 'Ulysses' and 'The Two Voices'.

November A letter by John Kemble refers to 'St Simeon Stylites'. 'Tithon' had been begun when 'Ulysses' was written, and may have been completed by this time.

December

3 (Tues) T thanks Monckton Milnes for his letter, and is delighted to hear that he is going to publish his Greek impressions. He requests M to make arrangements with Moxon to send him a copy on publication (*Memorials of a Tour in Some Parts of Greece, Chiefly Poetical*, 1834).

9 Henry Hallam invites T to accompany him in his carriage at his son's funeral. He has yet to hear that the ship bearing his coffin has left Trieste.

30 Henry Hallam writes to say that the ship has arrived sooner than expected. (The coffin was landed at Dover, and transported in a cortège – hearse and three coaches – drawn by sixteen black horses to Clevedon Court, home of AH's maternal grandfather Sir Abraham Elton.) He urges Alfred to support Emily, and not to give way to grief. T and his sister Mary are at the Rawnsleys' for dinner and dancing.

1834

3 January AH is buried in the family tomb, in the chancel of Clevedon Church, near Clevedon Court, his mother's early home. Tennant is present during 'New Year Revels' at Somersby.

14 February T informs Henry Hallam that he has failed to draw up a satisfactory memoir of Arthur's life and character for the collection of his writings which is to be published, but hopes that when time has brought the subject into focus he will write a tribute worthy of AH's 'high speculative endowments and comprehensive sympathies'.

26 April T writes to 'Christopher North', asking him not to suspect him of having 'one grain of sympathy' with John Lake, who has come to his (T's) defence in a satire ('mistermed') entitled 'Criticism and Taste'. He would rather shake hands with the critic against whom he wrote in a boisterous, petulant mood. Some of his poems were early compositions, full of faults, and he would hate to see them brought to public notice again in reply to the 'ravings' of the 'unhappy coxcomb' Mr Lake.

June John Heath (formerly an Apostle, now an assistant tutor at Trinity College, Cambridge) comes to Somersby with his brother Douglas.

July Mrs T has to write an excuse for Emily, who has been invited to stay with the Hallams at Molesey Park near Kingston. From Kitlands near Dorking, where he is staying with the Heaths, T visits the Hallams and spends a sad evening with them. Continuing his stay with the Heaths, he is taken to Worthing; a trip to Brighton is suggested, but he prefers to walk in wooded valleys near Leith Hill. A hundred copies of *Remains in Verse and Prose of Arthur Henry Hallam,* with a memoir by his father, are published for private circulation. Whether T is sent copies or given them – his stay in the south, including a period at Molesey Park, extends into August – is not clear; he sends a copy to his grandfather in July. At the end of the month Tennant writes to T at Kitlands: he knows he has no hope of winning Cecilia, and has assured Mrs T that he will not renew his attentions provided he may continue visiting Somersby as a friend.

21 August At Somersby T is 'so unwell as to be almost a prisoner in the house'. (He has been reading Racine, Molière, and Victor Hugo. Subsequently perhaps he dips into F. D. Maurice's *Eustace Conway* – in great disfavour at Kitlands – and Sterling's *Arthur Coningsby,* which he finds 'dreary'.)

September He has written 'Sir Galahad'. He writes the lines 'Thy rosy lips are soft and sweet' for Rosa Baring's birthday on the 23rd, the first of his flirtatious verses to her. She lives at Harrington Hall, and his friendly with the Sellwoods and the Somersby Ts.

October He asks Spedding's advice on 'Love thou thy land' (the text of which he sends with variants), and tells Tennant that he is copying out 'Morte d'Arthur'. Perhaps after taking Emily to Molesey Park on the 13th (she meets Richard Jesse, her future husband, there, and becomes one of the family, accompanying the Hallams to Wimpole Street, and staying with them until February), T visits the Wye valley; cf. *In Memoriam*, xix, and 'Tears, idle tears' (*The Princess*, iv), which came to him 'on the yellowing autumn-tide at Tintern Abbey'.

December John Heath is at Somersby for Christmas. (Subsequently he and Mary T became engaged; his breaking of the engagement in 1837 ended his friendship with the Ts.)

1835

15 February T intimates to his friend James Spedding that he would like to visit him in the Lake District. He has sold his Chancellor's Medal (for £15) to that end.

March (early) He tells JS that John Stuart Mill is to review his poems favourably in a new magazine, but does not wish the reading public to be reminded of his poetry. (After Croker's review he did not dare to publish for nine years.) His brother Charles, having inherited his great-uncle Samuel Turner's large estate (and adopted his surname, in accordance with his benefactor's wishes) has given up his Tealby curacy for the living at Grasby (the advowson of which had come to him), and now occupies a big house (where his grandmother spent her early years) in Caistor.

13 March T takes his sisters Matilda and Cecilia to Mablethorpe for a week or a fortnight. (During the month T visits Charles, finds Caistor and the surrounding country unattractive, and later describes his brother as 'the first man in the place, an owner of books and pictures, a watercloset with a recumbent Venus in it, and a house with a stone front'.)

9 April A dinner-party, followed by dancing, is held by the Ts. Emily, who had learnt to waltz in London and introduced the dance to her family and friends, notices Sophy Rawnsley, 'the lightest and most indefatigable dancer' she has ever seen; 'Alfred is delighted with her.' (Emily Sellwood is another visitor to Somersby this spring.)

April (the last three weeks) T is the guest of the Speddings at Mirehouse, Bassenthwaite, where he meets Edward FitzGerald, who becomes his lifelong friend. Fitz sees several of T's new poems, including 'Dora' (derived considerably from a story by Miss Mitford), and hears him read 'Michael' and other poems by Wordsworth with admiration. T reads also from Milton, saying that 'Lycidas' is 'a test of any reader's poetic instinct', and from Keats, who 'would have been, if he had lived, the greatest of us all'. The weather is wet and cold, and T, finding it 'Arctic', is 'grumpy'.

May (early) JS takes his friends to stay at Ambleside, where he has to leave them a few days. T discusses 'Morte d'Arthur' with Fitz, who buys him a copy of Wordsworth's recently published *Yarrow Revisited, and Other Poems*. (Whether T actually saw W at Rydal Mount is uncertain: he resisted JS's wish to take him, but the visitors' book shows that they called, possibly after Fitz had left, when T and JS returned to Mirehouse.) During their last two days at Ambleside, JS introduces them to Hartley Coleridge. T intends to call on Brookfield at Maltby (where he is curate) on his way back to Somersby.

2 July Fitz writes, offering to send T money occasionally if he will accept it; he has bought him a copy of Dante.

4 July George T dies at Usselby, to which he had retired in 1833, making way for his son Charles at Bayons Manor. (At the end of the month the King's Licence is issued for Charles to assume the name and arms of d'Eyncourt. For several years he is preoccupied with the building of a new Bayons Manor, representing on a grand scale and in lavish detail the medieval evolution of a manorial moated castle, with a high dining-hall to seat two hundred.

George's funeral achieved spectacular impressiveness. Not one of the Somersby Ts attended it, and his will created much ill-feeling among relatives. He had left the bulk of his possessions to his son Charles, but, following his declared intentions, he bequeathed the whole of his own inheritance, which was considerable, to his elder son's family. Mrs T received nothing beyond the £200 p.a. which came from Frederick's legacy, he as the eldest receiving the largest share – most of it a life interest in the Clayton estate at Grimsby. Charles (Tennyson) Turner, being already well endowed, received nothing. Alfred's chief inheritance was a manor and an estate at Grasby, the whole being adequate to keep anyone comfortable with good management; he still received £100 p.a. from his aunt Elizabeth Russell.)

During the month John Stuart Mill's defensive but discriminating review of T's 1830 and 1833 volumes appears in *The London Review*.

1 September According to Charles Tennyson d'Eyncourt, Alfred has been so 'violent' about the terms of the will that Mr and Mrs Bourne, with whom he has been staying at Dalby, have sent him away. (He may have visited Boulogne for two days.)

Autumn He spends an evening at the Cock Tavern, opposite Temple Bar (i.e. in Fleet Street), with JS, Fitz, and the latter's old Trinity friend William Makepeace Thackeray.

1836

19 April T is staying with his Cambridge friend Monckton Milnes at the latter's home in Bawtry. They had been disappointed not to find Brookfield at his parents' home in Southbourne, Sheffield, the previous day, and hope he can join them at Bawtry on Wednesday (the next day).

2 May They leave Bawtry for Fryston Hall, the home of the Milneses near Doncaster.

24 May Charles Turner marries Louisa, the youngest daughter of Henry Sellwood, a Horncastle solicitor. (After being a volunteer, Sellwood had thought of becoming an army officer; he then lived an expensive life as a country gentleman in Berkshire, before deciding to qualify for a profession. His wife, sister of the Arctic explorer John Franklin – a native of Spilsby, knighted in 1829 – had died in 1816.) At the wedding in Horncastle, Alfred T is the best man, and Emily Sellwood, the eldest of the three sisters, a bridesmaid. (T's poem 'The Bridesmaid' suggests that they fell in love on this occasion.) His brother Charles was so nervous that he took opium with disastrous consequences; the addiction from which he suffered at Tealby returned, resulting in Louisa's breakdown and their separation until 1849, one reason for the long deferment of T's marriage.

June

7 (Tues) He informs Mr Sellwood that he will be happy to dine with him on Saturday.

11 He, Frederick, and Mary T dine at the Sellwoods', where the party is gathered to bid farewell to Sir John Franklin, who is leaving to take up his appointment as Governor of Tasmania. His dark attractive orphaned niece Catherine Franklin is also present, and T slightly unnerves her when he sits by her as she plays the piano.

14 or 15 T sends 'St Agnes' Eve' ('written some three years back') in response to a request from Brookfield for *The Keepsake*.

October (end) In wintry weather T writes to Milnes, hoping to visit him at Fryston ('Freezetown') in December.

November 'St Agnes' Eve' appears in *The Keepsake*, an annual edited by Lady Emmeline Stuart Wortley. Although T had vowed never to contribute to such publications, he gave way when he heard from Brookfield (who contributed a sonnet) that her sister had written to him and said Lady Wortley was beautiful.

December When Milnes asks him for a contribution to *The Tribute*, after assuring the editor, the Marquis of Northampton, that he could expect something, T takes umbrage, and explains why he has acted against his principles in contributing to *The Keepsake*. He is thinking of joining Frederick, now in Italy.

1837

8 or 9 January T tries wittily to appease Milnes (who, offended by his previous letter, has threatened to send his copy of 'Anacaona' to the Marquis), and promises to forward or bring something for *The Tribute*. He has also persuaded his brother Charles to contribute.

March (?) He sends Milnes an expanded version, which has given him great trouble, of 'Oh! that 'twere possible', a poem arising from AH's death, and vows he will have nothing more to do with such books as annuals. 'So never ask me', he concludes.

During March, April, and May he spends much time in London and its vicinity searching for a house, the rectory at Somersby having been requisitioned as expected. For his own visits to London, and those of other members of his family, he rents rooms at 12 Mornington Crescent. For their future home he secures Beech Hill House, with its own park and gardens, at High Beech in the Epping Forest area, three miles from Waltham Cross. He meets many old friends in London, smokes as heavily as ever, composes poetry, often without writing it down, and becomes acquainted with Samuel Rogers. They 'seem to have taken a great fancy to each other', JS notes.

April

3 (Mon) JS dines with T at the Cock Tavern (cf. 'Will Waterproof's Lyrical Monologue'; another dining-house favoured by T during his unsettled pre-marriage years is Bertolini's near Leicester Square). Influenza prevents T from visiting the Kembles.

10 It is wintry, and T, who has been reading Charles Lyell's *Principles of Geology*, writes his lines 'The tenth of April! is it not?'

11 He attends a masque by John Oxenford which is based on Pope's *The Rape of the Lock*.

During the spring he meets Milnes, Monteith, Brookfield, and other friends in London; he gives a reading of 'The Two Voices' in Edmund Lushington's rooms.

May He spends much of his time buying the main requirements, and ensuring that other preparations are made, for the occupation of Beech Hill House.

June The Ts leave Somersby for their new home. Before their departure they take leave of friends and relatives. T walks with his brother Charles from Caistor to Bayons Manor, to pay their respects and view its seigneurial progress. With Cecilia they drive rather late one evening to their aunt Mary's at Dalby. After supper they proceed to the Rawnsleys at Halton Holgate, their last call before leaving Lincolnshire.

T writes 'The Queen of the Isles', and forwards it to JS for anonymous publication in *The Times*, 'or some paper with a circulation', to coincide with Queen Victoria's accession to the throne on the 20th.

('A known landskip is to me an old friend, that continually talks to me of my own youth and half-forgotten things, and does more for me than many an old friend that I know', T writes later to Emily Sellwood. Some of his more particular thoughts on leaving Lincolnshire are to be found in *In Memoriam*, c–ciii.)

31 July Leigh Hunt expresses delight that T should 'find anything to like' in his verses, especially 'Paganini', and hopes he will send a sonnet or fragment of verse for *The Monthly Repository*, of which he has become editor.

T's responsibilities at Beech Hill House take up much of his time, and his unpractical mother is dependent on him. He and other members of his family like to get away from a rather disorderly home (too noisy for T, who escapes to London when he can, staying at Mornington Crescent or with friends).

Christmas The Ts receive a turkey, a pork pie, and sausages from Mrs Rawnsley, and Mrs T finds it 'gratifying . . . to taste again good, wholesome, dear old Lincolnshire Pork'.

Hallam T's memoir of his father includes a letter in which Gladstone recalls meeting T for the first time 'about the year 1837, when he called on me in Carlton Gardens. This was an unexpected honour, for I had no other tie with him than having been in earlier life the friend of his friend, to whom he afterwards erected so splendid a literary monument.'

1838

28 January T writes to Mrs Rawnsley, hoping that she, Sophy, and Mr R will find time to visit them; life near 'this great black Babylon', he tells her, is artificial and cold; people are hospitable but not 'in a good old-fashioned way so as to do one's feelings any good'.

19 March T leaves Cambridge for Epping, after a week there. J. W. Blakesley reports that he complains of nervousness, and asks how it can be otherwise when 'he smokes the strongest and most stinking tobacco out of a small blackened clay pipe on an average nine hours every day'.

April Edward FitzGerald reports a visit from T in London: 'very droll, and very wayward: and much sitting up of nights till two and three in the morning with pipes in our mouths: at which good hour we would get Alfred to give us some of his magic music, which he does between growling and smoking'.

11 April Cecilia reports very cold weather, and the visits of many Lincolnshire friends to Beech Hill House; they include her cousin Louis Fytche, Miss Rawnsley, and Anne Sellwood, who has gone for her health with Mary T to Guernsey. The night before they left, they had had great fun, Alfred amusing them all the time with his impersonations.

April (later) T probably visits Emily Sellwood at Horncastle. Afterwards, it seems, from the high road through Hagworthingham, he sees the tops of the elms on the Somersby lawn 'beginning to kindle into green'. He remembers sitting with her there when he had first come from London three years ago, but earlier in the year than now. The memory is 'fresh and pleasant'; she wore a silk pelisse, and he thinks he read a book with her. (For this Lincolnshire visit, cf. *In Memoriam* cxv, a recollection of April 1838 according to the poet's grandson: Charles T, *Alfred Tennyson*.

14 May T is in London again, hoping to visit Windsor with Fitz.

6 June From Torquay, in the briefest of letters (saying he needs a frank), he tells Milnes that he likes his recently published poems.

Late July or early August Edmund Lushington, who was elected Fellow of Trinity College, Cambridge, in 1834, is appointed Professor of Greek at Glasgow University.

Autumn T visits Torquay alone, and writes 'Audley Court', the background of which is suggested by Abbey Park.

November Emily Sellwood stays at Beech Hill House. (She and T probably became engaged in the spring.)

December T sends John Forster a sovereign towards the fund he is helping to raise in aid of Leigh Hunt.

During the year T often calls on Thackeray and Fitz's friend John Allen, at their homes in Coram Street. He has probably met Thomas Carlyle of 5 Cheyne Row, Chelsea, German scholar and author of *The French Revolution*; both are members of the club founded by John Sterling in 1838. They may have breakfasted with Monckton Milnes at 26 Pall Mall.

1839

February Moxon's offer of £60 for a preface to a life of Beaumont and Fletcher is declined by T.

23 March T and his sister Emily have gone with their mother to London for a month or six weeks. Cecilia, who is ill, hopes to join them in 'about a week or ten days'.

10 July He writes to Emily Sellwood, reporting a violent thunderstorm 'the other night', with a huge fire-ball passing close to High Beech and exploding 'like fifty batteries of cannon'.

July (later) T moves on from Aberystwyth to Barmouth, which he prefers for its 'Mablethorpelike' breakers, its sandhills and high craggy cliffs, and its long estuary (cf. *In Memoriam*, lxxxvi, composed at this time). The Llanberis lakes, near which he writes 'Edwin Morris', are the 'most beautiful thing' he sees during this visit to Wales.

24 October T's correspondence continues a metaphysical discussion with Emily Sellwood. (Relations between the Sellwoods and the Ts are strained, partly because Charles Turner's return to opium has led to a separation between him and his wife Louisa, Emily's sister, partly because T's unsettled habits and apparent lack of ambition have sown suspicion; even more perhaps, because, with mental derangement and outbreaks of epilepsy in his family, he is becoming obsessed with fear of hereditary consequences should he marry. His metaphysics seem evasive, but he asks Emily to trust him.)

23 November He is in London with FitzGerald, who provides dinner for him and two or three others: 'soles, two boiled fowls, and an Apple Tart – cheese, etc. After this plenty of smoking.'

25 November Fitz and his friends want T to publish another volume, but he is 'too lazy and wayward'. He has 'fine things' in a large butcher's account book (cf. 2 Mar 1842 and 28 Feb 1849).

During the year Frederick T marries Maria Giuliotti, daughter of the chief magistrate of Siena, and settles in Florence.

1840

January T is in Lincolnshire part of the month; perhaps he visits Horncastle. He had talked of going to Grasby, but his brother Charles is at High Beech during his absence. The Ts are about to move to Tunbridge Wells, which has been recommended by their doctor because (in Cecilia's words) 'the air is so dry and the place so high'.

February
The move takes place during this month. T does not look forward to living in the new house, which is like a mouse-trap, lacking room for his books, which he fears he will have to sell.
15 (Sat) Returning from a new play by 'poor Leigh Hunt', Fitz finds T installed in his lodgings, and very nervously ill.
17 T is still with him. Fitz ascribes his illness to heredity and incessant smoking.
Later in the month T joins his mother, who has been ill and gone to Cheltenham (probably to avoid the disturbance and discomfort of the removal). Tunbridge Wells is his 'abomination'.

April (?) He may have spent some time with the Lushingtons at Park House, Boxley, near Maidstone. (See the parenthesis which follows 28 Aug.)

May (?) It seems that T stayed at Mablethorpe during this month. He had broken his engagement, and it could have been at this time (or in January) that Emily Sellwood's relatives were rude to him at Horncastle.

June (early) At Warwick, after journeying from Lincoln via Leicester, T, wearing his eye-glass by chance as the mail-coach drives in, catches sight of Fitz walking towards Leamington. They make excursions to Kenilworth Castle and Stratford, and visit Warwick Castle. From Coventry he travels by train to London, and writes 'Godiva'. About this time, or later, he sends Emily Sellwood a copy of his ballad 'Edward Gray'.

July (?) T stays a fortnight (not as a patient, Spedding writes to John Allen) at 'a madhouse' (near High Beech; established by Dr Matthew Allen at Fair Mead, where T's brother Septimus is a voluntary patient).

Late July or early August Carlyle finds Matthew Allen and T smoking in his garden; they have been an hour or two with his wife Jane, who had not met T before.

August

26 (Wed) T arrives in Southampton, where he stays at the Castle Inn. His friend W. H. Brookfield, a curate there, takes him to Charles Elton's, probably to introduce the latter's daughter Jane (AH's cousin), to whom he is engaged.

27 T dines with Charles Elton. (On one of these visits he puts his hand on Mr Elton's head, saying 'You must have done many a foolish thing in your time with that great big bump of benevolence of yours.')

28 After walking in Southampton during the afternoon with Brookfield's father (also on a visit), he leaves at 9 p.m. for Le Havre. (He changes his mind, and stays in England.)

(Perhaps after the Southampton visit he stays at Park House.'I believe the first time he visited me in my own house was in the summer of 1840 when he came to stay for a few days', Edmund Lushington wrote: cf. Hallam T's memoir of his father, I, p. 201.)

September T brings Edmund L to Tunbridge Wells, where Lushington meets Cecilia for the first time. (Whether T wrote any more letters in 1840 to Emily Sellwood after this is uncertain. Henry Sellwood forbad the correspondence, which was not renewed until 1850, though Emily was still in love with T. The poem 'Love and Duty' may have grown from his awareness of this. Later she referred to their 'ten years' separation'.)

Early November (?) T is at Trinity, Cambridge, where, with Brookfield, Trench, Milnes, Henry Lushington and others, he sups in Merivale's rooms. For some time there has been a campaign for the election of the college candidate Lord Lyttelton (whom Brookfield had tutored) as High Steward of the University; the poll closes on the 12th, when Lord Lyndhurst is returned.

23 November T has given Matthew Allen £900 to invest in a 'pyroglyph' industry, a process of wood-carving by machinery for the manufacture of furniture for churches and homes. In return he receives an insurance policy for £2000 on Allen's life, with the promise of further insurance if he invest more, and interest at 5 per cent. (As time passes the T investment grows, involving other members of the family, his mother and Charles included. For this T is to sell his Grasby estate, and part with the £500 legacy he has received from AH's aunt.)

1841

January Part of the time T is with Fitz in London. Dalby House, home of his aunt and uncle, Mary and John Bourne, is burnt down on the 5th.

22 February He has been living at Mablethorpe for a month. Under pressure to have his poems published in the United States, T informs Charles Stearns Wheeler, friend of Emerson and Lowell, that he will first revise what is worth correcting in his two published volumes, then republish them with several new poems, and send copies to him and the publishers Little and Brown, to do as they choose with them.

March Fitz informs Frederick T that he has seen Alfred once or twice, and that sometimes he is to be found with his 'little bit of dirty pipe', and a 'particularly dirty vellum book of MSS on the sofa', at 8 Charlotte Street (not far from his own London home); he hints also at returns to Allen's High Beech asylum. At one of Milnes's breakfasts, T meets Henry Crabb Robinson and the 'author of unreadable books', Robert Browning. On the 29th he encounters Brookfield by chance in the National Gallery. (Whether he visited Torquay during the month or some time in 1842 – as Hallam T indicates in his memoir: I, p. 215 – is uncertain.)

12 May T gives 7 Charlotte Street as the address of his London lodgings.

August He returns from a week in Paris, after visiting Rotterdam and Amsterdam. He spends some time with the Lushingtons at Park House, where he meets George Venables and George Granville Bradley.

26 August James Brown, the American publisher, sees T briefly.

19 September T writes from Otley, Yorkshire, to Edmund Lushington; he enjoyed meeting his brother Henry at High Beech. The other day he was led to Bolton Abbey by a note to Wordsworth's poem 'The White Doe of Rylstone'.

7 October Jane Elton is upset to learn that Emily T is to marry 'a boy in the Navy, *supposed* to be a Midshipman'.

24 October Charles Turner writes to his uncle Charles d'Eyncourt, supporting his sisters' request that he should release £2000 from their inheritance for investment in the pyroglyph venture.

November (late) From 19 Charlotte Street Fitz writes, telling Bernard Barton that T and he 'pass some hours together every day and night: with pipes and Brandy and Water'. T is a 'great fellow' but 'he is ruining himself by mismanagement and neglect of all kinds'. (Fitz knows about T's speculations, and has already expressed 'much fear for poor Alfred's money'. He thinks he smokes 'twelve hours out of the twenty-four'.)

24 December 'Alfred Tennyson, my neighbour, is getting better', Fitz writes, and advises him to 'go down to his friends for Xmas'. T seems 'half inclined'.

December (end) He spends Christmas at Boxley Hall, to which his family has recently moved. They are near the Lushingtons at Park House; Edmund L spends much of his short holiday from Glasgow with them.

1842

January Fitz travels with T from Gravesend to London, and pastes a silhouette of him in his copy of T's 1832 *Poems*.

24 January T and two of his sisters attend the wedding of Emily T and Richard Jesse, a naval lieutenant (commissioned 23 Nov 1841); T gives the bride away. (After the wedding T takes his sisters to London, where they lodge in the home of a violent madman, who cries out murder in the night and has to be put in a strait waistcoat. T is so upset by this that he spends a month at Fair Mead under Allen's surveillance.)

March

2 (Wed) He has returned to London, where Fitz takes him 'by violence' to Moxon's in order to settle the publication of his long-delayed new volume of poems, most of them culled from what Fitz called 'The Butcher's Book'.

17 T is at Spedding's, 60 Lincoln's Inn Fields, correcting proofs. He thinks the poems detestable in print, and regrets allowing them to be published.

26 Fitz takes him to Dulwich, hoping the Gallery will not be closed for Easter. (In a letter to Fitz, written probably early in July, T recalls the days spent at Dulwich, and says he has not had 'a good day, a perfect white day, for years'.)

14 April (Thurs) Samuel Rogers thanks T for thinking of him (as a guest?), and invites him to breakfast on Saturday or Sunday or both; he will be delighted to see him at ten o'clock.

19 April T and Venables have tea with the Brookfields (married in Nov) in Jermyn Street.

9 May 'Have faith and all things will be more than well', Matthew Allen writes 'affectionately' to T.

14 May *Poems* is published in two volumes, the first containing a revised selection from the 1830 and 1832 volumes, with a few written about 1833, the second consisting of new poems. (T sends copies to C. S. Wheeler, who arranges publication with William D. Ticknor & Co. of Boston. He received $150 for copyright.)

July A reviewer (Francis Garden) for *The Christian Remembrancer* sees 'positive progress' in *Poems*, but tends to regret T's remoteness from life and the contemporary world.

6 July T attends the festival of the Maidstone Mechanics' Institute in the grounds of Park House (cf. the Prologue to *The Princess*). (Shortly afterwards he hears news, which makes him question Allen's intentions.)

July (end) and early August He is with Henry Lushington and two of Henry's sisters at Eastbourne, where he writes to Aubrey de Vere, saying he will be *highly honoured* to receive a copy of Henry Taylor's new verse-drama *Edwin the Fair* from the author.

August Granville Bradley meets T several times at Park House. Fitz hears that T's poems have sold well, especially at Cambridge.

17 August Rogers writes to tell T that 'very few things, if any, have ever thrilled' him as much as his *Poems*.

September Writing anonymously in *The Quarterly Review*, John Sterling emphasizes the need for the 'right imaginative use' of the contemporary world in poetry, and finds it in the best of T's poems, which are 'among the richest of our recent literature'. (The editor, J. G. Lockhart, anxious to atone for Croker's review of 1833, had invited Sterling to review any book he pleased, expecting him to choose *Poems*. Croker is highly annoyed.)

During the early part of the month T, intent on accepting Aubrey de Vere's invitation to western Ireland, is detained at Boxley with inquiries arising from news reaching him that the wood-carving company in which he and his family were heavily invested is threatened with failure. Not meeting de Vere as arranged, he sets off for Ireland alone.

8 September He writes to Edmund Lushington, probably from Dublin; he has crossed from Liverpool, and leaves that night for Limerick. 'What with ruin in the distance and hypochondriacs in the foreground', he feels 'very crazy'. (Before leaving he called to see Moxon, and found he had gone to the Pyrenees with Wordsworth's two sons. Five hundred of his books have been sold, and Moxon's brother thought he had made a sensation. He is to be the guest of the de Veres at Curragh Chase, County Limerick.)

September (mid) He writes from Killarney to Aubrey de Vere; he has visited the Ballybunion caves, but bad weather has made it impossible to enter the finest of them.

23 September He travels from Cork to Bristol.

October Monckton Milnes writes on T's *Poems* in *The Westminster Review*, taking the usual Apostolic line that art should relate to the modern world.

10 October Edmund Lushington and Cecilia T are married at Boxley, Charles Turner officiating at the wedding-ceremony. Alfred gives the bride away, and celebrates with champagne.

15 October Hearing that Dr Allen has persuaded Septimus at Fair Mead to promise him £1000 for investment, T writes to Mrs Allen, informing her that her husband has already received about £8000 from 'our family', and that his mother and sisters are now dependent on his brother Charles.

7 December Thomas Carlyle (no lover of poetry in general) writes to T, praising his poems, some of which he has re-read and means to read 'over and over' until they are his.

27 December T dines with the Carlyles. Thomas finds he is 'a right hearty talker' and 'one of the powerfullest *smokers*' he has ever 'worked along with in that department'.

1843

23–4 January T is at Mablethorpe. (The length of his stay is conjectural; he is obliged to return to London 'in a hurry', probably in February.)

4 March Allen writes to Frederick T, telling him he has ruined himself to save the T family, and will sell 'every stick and stave' to pay T '*this day*'. '*Come up*! you must save something', he adds. (Any efforts he made were unavailing. It is not clear when FT came to see him.)

10 March Charles Dickens sends copies of his works to T in homage to the 'Truth and Beauty' of his writings.

April Spedding's favourable review of *Poems* in *The Edinburgh Review* (delayed because of his visit to America) emphasizes the increase of humanity in T's poetry, and his concern for the prime duties of man.

27 April T dines at Devonshire Terrace with Dickens; Thackeray and Fitz are present. Afterwards they have 'a round game of cards and mulled claret'.

4 May Frederick T leaves Boxley for London.

6 May T (now proof-reading for a reprint of *Poems*) hopes that FT has called on Fitz. He is afraid that his brother will 'get into some absurd scrape' over his own financial involvement with Allen, and wishes therefore that Fitz can persuade him to consult a good lawyer before taking action.

17 September T writes to Aubrey de Vere from St Leonards-on-Sea, where he is staying 'with the Lushingtons'.

November (early) Unable to afford Boxley Hall, the Ts move to 6 Belle Vue Place, Cheltenham. Their new home is much smaller, but the family is reduced in size as well as means. Emily and Cecilia are married; Edward, in a home for the insane (at York) since 1833, is to remain there for the rest of his life; and, if they have not already left, Septimus and Arthur – the one after being a patient at Fair Mead, the other after voluntary treatment in Scotland for alcoholism – are to leave towards the end of the year to join FT in Italy, where they can live cheaply. Fitz sees T in London, on his way to Cheltenham, never looking 'so hopeless' and ill; his younger brother Horatio is with him, seeming 'rather unused to the planet'. T accepts an invitation to dine with Samuel Rogers before making his way to Cheltenham.

December Edmund Lushington has taken out an insurance for £2000 on Allen's life for T's benefit. After his family has settled in their new home, T enters a hydropathic hospital at Prestbury, near Cheltenham.

1844

2 February T informs Fitz that he has been in a hydropathy establishment 'upwards of two months'. 'The perpetual panic and horror of the last two years had steeped my nerves in poison: now I am left a beggar but I am or shall be shortly somewhat better off in nerves.' He has had four crises, and much poison 'has come out of me'. Too poor to make trips to London, he thinks of moving when he is cured to Italy, where his three brothers can live happily on eight shillings a day. (The statement said to be made by Carlyle that Fitz lent T £300 annually 'for many years' when he was poor lacks confirmation. It seems quite unlikely that Fitz could afford such a sum, nor was T penniless; he still received £100 p.a. from his aunt, and income from his publications was far from negligible.)

June He leaves the hydro (where he has had ten crises) to stay at Cheltenham with his mother, after her visit to Cecilia in Scotland.

June (end) He is staying at Aberystwyth.

July
8 (Mon) He is at Barmouth.
16 He leaves Barmouth for Caernarvon,and regrets his inability to see Venables at Builth for that reason.
29 He writes to Edmund Lushington, and tells him he has climbed Snowdon three times, finding the ascent much easier than walking on level ground.
30 He travels to London, where he intends to stay two or three days, hoping to see an exhibition of art-work designed for the interior and exterior of the new Houses of Parliament.

August (early) He lodges in Henry Lushington's rooms, 2 Mitre Court Buildings, the Temple. Carlyle expects to see him. R. H. Horne wishes to include an engraving of T's portrait in the second edition of his *The New Spirit of the Age*, and T, who is calling on the artist Samuel Laurence, promises to arrange that his chalk-sketch is sent.

7 August T informs Carlyle that he has been too feverish to call, and that he must go to Kent the next day if he is strong enough. For three days he has lived on eighteen lemons.

9 August He attends a dinner-party given by Thackeray.

10 October Fitz informs Frederick T that 'Alfred is reported to be still at Park House, where he has been sojourning for two months'. On this day (or a little earlier), however, he is at

Carlyle's from about two in the afternoon until late in the evening, when he is dismissed with 'Macpherson's Farewell', the tune M played on his way to the gallows, where he discovered he had no friend. Carlyle notices T's face grow darker, and his lip quiver slightly, at the thought.

26 October In a letter to Fitz, Carlyle refers to this meeting on an 'unforgettable' day, and states that T ought to have a Civil List pension of £200 p.a.

15 November From Cheltenham, where he and his family have moved to 10 St James's Square, T requests Moxon to send him two anonymous books, *Vestiges of the Natural History of Creation* (by R. Chambers) and *Modern Painters* (the first volume, by John Ruskin).

30 November He has been much impressed by Hariet Martineau's first two articles on mesmerism in *The Athenaeum* (23 and 30 Nov), and will forward them to his aunt Elizabeth if she wishes.

1845

January

14 (Tues) T has heard news of Dr Allen's death. (Thanks to Edmund Lushington, he can now look forward with a sense of security.)

16 He leaves Cheltenham for London, where Fitz finds him looking much better, though almost a valetudinarian.

29 Fitz reports that T is drinking a bottle of wine daily. The same day (most probably) T and Moxon call at Carlyle's home in Chelsea. In her husband's absence Jane Carlyle provides pipes and tobacco, and brandy and water (as C, who has 'missed the man he likes best', would have done), with a 'deluge' of tea. T smokes for three hours, 'talking like an angel'. When C returns at midnight he finds Jane '*alone* in an atmosphere of tobacco so thick that you might have cut it with a knife'.

31 T dines with Spedding, Lushington (Henry?), Moxon, and others at Samuel Rogers'. Henry Crabb Robinson discusses Goethe with him. Caroline Norton, an admirer of T's poetry, arrives late.

3 February T writes to Richard Howitt from Cheltenham, asking him, if he is staying with them, to convey his regards to William and Mary Howitt, and say how much he would like to know them.

6 February Carlyle informs Fitz that T, 'the fiery Son of Gloom', left London, he thinks, on Sunday (the 2nd).

April In the middle of the month T returns to London, lodging at 7 Charlotte Street.

17 (Thurs) Aubrey de Vere calls on T, and finds him 'at first much out of spirits'. T reads some 'beautiful Elegies', and complains of some writer in *Fraser's Magazine* who had criticized the 'foolish facility' of Tennysonian poetry. After visiting the House of Commons, de Vere returns, and listens to T's 'magnificent Elegies' until 1 a.m.

18 T reads his manuscript poetry to Tom Taylor and de Vere, who (after walking with T to his lawyer's) returns, and hears him read from 'The University of Women' (published as *The Princess*). Brookfield calls the same day, and invites T to dinner. T arrives at five, and meets Kate and Julia Hallam; at T's invitation Moxon comes, and stays till six. Brookfield and T smoke till 1 a.m.

19 Brookfield, Thackeray, and Tom Taylor call in the morning. After dinner, B finds T at Moxon's, where they smoke until nearly 2 a.m.

29 T dines at the Sterling Club with JS, B, Venables, Merivale, Trench, two Spring Rices, and others.

May

4 (Sun) De Vere takes T, 'murmuring sore', to see Wordsworth at Hampstead. The door is opened by Rogers, who says, 'Ah, you did not come up the hill to see me!' T complains because he has failed to elicit any enthusiastic response from W (on the subject of scarlet trees on a tropical island).

6 T dines with W (who is friendly) and others at Moxon's. (After another dinner at M's during the month, the two poets establish more cordial relations in the drawing-room; later W describes T as 'decidedly the first of our living poets'.)

9 T smokes at de Vere's, and speaks with pleasure of his meeting with W.

10 He reads from 'The University of Women' to de Vere, and denounces exotics in poetry, which should 'reflect the time and place'.

11 De Vere calls on T and spends three hours with him and Fitz, trying to persuade T to come to Hither Green. On the way they walk through Greenwich Park, and T is delighted with the landscape view and colouring.They have a 'merry' dinner, and talk beyond midnight.

Towards the end of the month T goes to Eastbourne, 'to consider the sea from the top of Beachy Head', Fitz writes.

12 June He is still there, Fitz believes.

July

1 (Tues) Aubrey de Vere, driving into the city from Hampstead, meets T, who is little pleased to see him, and living, it seems, 'in a mysterious sort of way on the Hampstead Road, bathing and learning Persian'.

3 A friend persuades T to visit the Cartoons, an exhibition at Westminster Hall showing frescoes designed for the House of Lords.

14 De Vere calls on T, who rails against 'the whole system of society', and says he is miserable.

16 Again out of spirits, T tells de Vere that he can 'no longer bear to be knocked about the world, and that he must marry and find love and peace or die'. He is 'very angry about a very favourable review of him', Aubrey writes, and complains much about growing old and his life being 'thrown away for want of a competence and retirement'.

August (mid) He is again at Eastbourne; he invites Moxon and Laurence down. Edmund Lushington stays a few days, and finds him busy with 'The University of Women', of which he has completed little more than the first part. He tells EL that he has included his marriage at the end of the AH elegies, the existence of which is a complete surprise to Lushington.

September

On the question of a Civil List pension for T, Sir Robert Peel, the Prime Minister, has sought the advice of Monckton Milnes, M.P., who sends him copies of 'Locksley Hall' and 'Ulysses', telling him that, if the pension is for literature, it should go to T; if for charity, to the dramatist Sheridan Knowles.

20 (Sat) T meets Mrs Carlyle at a private performance in Soho (by friends of Dickens) of Ben Jonson's *Every Man in His Humour*. (He does not recognise her, but atones by visiting her the next evening. Una Pope-Hennessy in her life of Dickens states that he attends the play again when performed before Prince Albert at St James's Theatre on 15 Nov.)

29 On returning to Cheltenham, T finds a letter from Henry Hallam with an enclosure from Sir Robert Peel, who tells Hallam that he proposes to recommend an annual pension of £200 for T. T accepts, and explains his delay in replying.

30 He calls on Brookfield in London, shows him Hallam's letter and Peel's proposal, and stays for dinner.

8 October Brookfield, Tom Taylor, and others dine with T.

October (mid) T has recently returned home from London. Lushington and Cecilia have stayed with them on their way to Glasgow. He is engaged to visit Henry Hallam at Wraxall Lodge near Bristol (he goes there at the end of the month).

(At Bayons Manor, where he is a guest, Edward Bulwer-Lytton has heard Charles Tennyson d'Eyncourt express surprise that his nephew, a man of means, should have been granted a pension. Bulwer incorporates his own views in a long satirical poem, *The New Timon*, which is to be published at the end of the year. He renews attacks on T's verse which he made in his review of Jan 1833, reviving memories of 'O Darling Room', a poem T wished to be forgotten. Peel is damned for feeding fat his 'puling Muse' while leaving Knowles to starve.)

1846

30 January Elizabeth Barrett tells Browning that T is ill, but has finished the second book of his 'fairy tale' called 'the "University", the university-members being all females'.

Early February (?) At his book-club in Cheltenham T catches sight of an editorial heading (deliberately exposed to excite local curiosity) which draws his attention to Bulwer's indictment in a reprint of the second part of *The New Timon*. After visiting John Forster (in London), who had corresponded with Bulwer on the authorship, and found his denials rather self-incriminating, T makes the most of his attacker's ridiculous dandyism and writes 'The New Timon, and the Poets', signing it 'Alcibiades', after the reader of the misanthropic Timon's epitaph at the end of Shakespeare's *Timon of Athens*. He gives Forster a copy, apparently without thought of publication.

18 February He has been persuaded to publish, and F sends him a proof-copy of his poem. T has sent him a second instalment of it.

28 February The poem (first instalment) appears in *Punch*. (Many are delighted; several newspaper and magazines side with T; and Bulwer continues to deny authorship of *The New Timon*. With Forster, however, he gave up his pose of innocence a year later, and the offending passages were removed from subsequent editions.)

7 March T's poem 'After-Thought' (later entitled 'Literary Squabbles') appears in *Punch*; signed 'Alcibiades' again, it expresses regret for 'pigmy' retaliation.

21 April T stands as godfather to Dickens' son (named Alfred D'Orsay Tennyson), but declines his invitation to accompany him to Switzerland.

May

1 (Fri) Elizabeth Barrett has heard (she informs Robert Browning) that T, after leaving London for a few days, has been seen at Venables' chambers (in the Temple).

3 His friends have persuaded him to draw his pension, Carlyle reports, adding, 'Surely no man has a right to be so lazy in this world.'

4 At T's, Fitz becomes tired of a two-hour discussion between the poet and Carlyle on the merits of this world and the next, and thinks C's arguments are wild and unreasonable.

5 He looks forward to 'a pint or two of fresh air' with

T at Richmond tomorrow, before 'a refreshing evening's entertainment' at C's.

9 T dines with the actor–manager Macready, a friend of Dickens and Forster.

12 At Moxon's he meets Browning and Joseph Severn, the artist who had been Keats's companion in Rome until his death. RB notices the charming way M takes care of T, a 'hazy kind of man, at least just after dinner'.

June With the poet Edmund Peel (Sir Robert's cousin) of Bonchurch, he roams over the downs in the Isle of Wight, and meets the dramatist James White (also of Bonchurch), a friend of Macready and Dickens; they row among the Needles.

July He spends a few weeks with the Lushingtons at Park House, and refreshes his memory for the setting of *The Princess*.

August

1 (Sat) He and Moxon leave London for Switzerland, staying the night at a fishmonger's in Ramsgate.

5 After staying in Bruges, and travelling via Liège to Cologne, they view the cathedral, and then proceed past Nonnenwerth and Drachenfels (with 'sad recollections' of 1832) to Koblenz.

8 By diligence from Basle to Lucerne.

10 By steamer to Weggis, where they hire a horse to ascend the Rigi. They sleep at the summit.

11 They are out at 4 a.m. to view the sunrise, and see the Jungfrau 'delicately pencilled' far off.

12 By boat to Alpnach, then by voiture up the valley of Sarnen to Lungern, then over the hills to Meiringen.

During the next few days they make their way to Grindelwald and Lauterbrunnen, where T writes most of the lyric 'Come down, O maid, from yonder mountain height' (*The Princess*, vii, 177–207). Seen as he descends from the Wengernalp, the Lauterbrunnen valley is one of 'the stateliest bits of landskip' he has ever seen.

18 They have reached Geneva.

23 They call on Dickens in Lausanne. D gives them 'some fine Rhine wine, and cigars innumerable'. He thinks T 'quite at home' and Moxon 'snobbish'.

31 They return to London.

(It seems that he spent much of the next three months at Cheltenham, where he works on *The Princess*.)

22 September Carlyle has heard from Moxon that T was in London the other day.

12 November From Cheltenham T writes to Fitz, chiefly on his tour in Switzerland. He has just obtained a copy of P. J. Bailey's *Festus*, and finds 'really *very grand* things' in it.

24 November From Tom Taylor's at Brompton, T writes to Mrs Burton at Somersby rectory, thanking her for the gift of violets which her daughter had picked. He does not wish to trouble her with reasons for not writing sooner; he is 'somewhat unwell', but people 'fête and dine' him every day.

December

5 (Sat) He is expected to dine with his publisher Moxon.
Before leaving London he visits William and Mary Howitt at Clapton, probably on the 13th and 14th. 'He spent a Sunday night at our house, when we sat talking until three in the morning. All the next day he remained with us in constant converse', MH wrote.

21 He leaves London to attend the tercentenary commemoration of the founding of Trinity College, Cambridge.

22 By special invitation of the Master, William Whewell, his old tutor, he attends the celebration dinner.

1847

24 January From Cheltenham he writes to Edward Rawnsley, elder son of T. H. Rawnsley. Mary T is in Paris; Matilda and Horatio are in Kent.

5 March T has considered Whewell's proposal that he should write an ode for the installation of Prince Albert as Chancellor of the University of Cambridge. He has made several efforts at it, but has to decline, though 'strongly sensible of the compliment' paid to him. (Wordsworth, ten days later, accepts the Prince Consort's invitation to write the ode for the occasion.)

16 April T is at Park House, after 'lying sick of more than one ailment' (he says) at Venables' chambers. He has come to bid farewell to Henry Lushington, who does not enjoy good health, and is going out to Malta 'as secretary to the Maltese government'. (His habit of 'coming unwashed and staying unbidden' is becoming a social embarrassment to the Lushington family, as Franklin tells Henry Hallam, AH's younger brother, not long afterwards.)

7 May 'Tennyson is now in London; ill and dispirited. He has finished his University of Women: and read me three Books of it the other night', Fitz writes, admitting that he slept during the reading. What he did hear was not wholly charming.

22 May T is at Umberslade Hall, south of Birmingham, undergoing hydropathic treatment for his continued nervous afflictions. He has not told his family where he is.

June For a number of weeks (possibly from the end of May, certainly into July) he spends much time checking proof-sheets for *The Princess*. On the 16th Charlotte Brontë sends him a copy of *Poems by Currer, Ellis, and Acton Bell* as an acknowledgment of the pleasure and profit they have derived from his works. Having sold only two copies in a year, they have decided to present a few.

July He may have left Umberslade Hall by the middle of the month.

July (late) After visiting two or three places in Warwickshire, he is back at Cheltenham, where he writes to Mrs Burton, telling her that he and his brother Charles will be godfathers to her little boy (born 6 July and christened Alfred). He is not publishing yet because the public is preoccupied with the General Election.

3 August For the election of University representatives he is at Trinity College, Cambridge, where he meets Thompson, Merivale, Brookfield, and other old friends.

24 August He is at Park House.

September (?) T's dinner-guests at 2 Mitre Court Buildings (Henry Lushington's rooms) include James White, Forster, and Leigh Hunt. (Thackeray and Tom Taylor have been invited.)

November From Mablethorpe he informs Moxon that he is 'putting the last touches' to *The Princess*. He will be staying there, he says, 'for about ten days'.

November (late) He undergoes hydrotherapy at Malvern under Dr Gully, who tells him he may suffer some paralysis at the age of fifty-five; sooner, if he continues smoking.

29 November T comes to London, and stays at the Prince of Wales, Leicester Place, having thought of going on to Kent.

December

3 (Fri) He takes lodgings at 42 Ebury Street for a week or two. (During the period he invites a few of his friends, including the Brookfields and Henry Hallam ('Harry'), to dinner. All works out well, the landlady making her sitting-room available for the ladies, after T had been dissuaded from dismantling his bedroom for the purpose.)

19 He visits the Carlyles.

25 *The Princess* is published. (Moxon had hoped to have it ready for pre-Christmas sales, but had been held up by T's revision.)

26 He spends the evening with the Carlyles (at their Chelsea home).

30 Carlyle writes as if T is still in London, 'dining daily till he is near dead'. He thinks T needs 'a task', which rhyming, 'in a Time like ours, will never furnish him'.

About the end of the year T writes to Fitz, saying he would like to go to Italy, but cannot find anyone to accompany him.

1848

1 January J. W. Marston in *The Athenaeum* finds much that is admirable in *The Princess*, but no advance. Like other critics, he feels the failure of T's art to reconcile discordant elements. (This is due to the artful disguise with which T presents a subject of contemporary importance. After a while, his work receives more favourable reviews.)

January (early) Harry Hallam buys T a gold pen, costing thirty shillings.

15 January Writing to Lord Monteagle from Ebury Street, T says he has missed Aubrey (de Vere), and hopes to see him before he leaves on Monday morning (the 17th, for Cheltenham).

Some time in January, or early February, Emily Sellwood, who moved with her father in 1847 to Hale Place near Farnham, Surrey, visits the Lushingtons. All believe T has gone to Italy, but he walks in before breakfast the next morning; she leaves as soon after as possible.

February By this time a second edition of *The Princess* has appeared, dedicated to Henry Lushington. T travels to Ireland, staying five weeks at Curragh Chase with Aubrey de Vere, who finds him unsettled, and wonders why he came, fearing he (T) does not like him. He is 'as simple as a child', and Aubrey finds he is growing very attached to him. 'He is all in favour of marriage, and indeed will not be right till he has some one to love him exclusively', de Vere writes. While at Curragh Chase T receives a letter from the author of *Festus*, who has been delighted to hear from Mary Howitt how much T admired the poem. She has quoted from T's letter to her in which he speaks of its 'Michael-Angelic' sublimity.

March (late) Such is T's desire to see grand waves and cliffs that he is sent to a cousin of the de Veres, the Knight of Kerry, on Valencia. Aubrey accompanies him part of the way; they sleep at Lord Monteagle's, and climb Knock Patrick, where the patron saint of Ireland, reaching the furthest point in his mission to the south-west, preached his famous sermon.

April (early) On the island of Valencia T sees huge Atlantic waves, and cliffs rising to a height of 600 feet or more. A Fenian follows him up a mountain to ask him if he is from France.

April (mid) He spends a few days at Killarney, where bugle echoes inspire 'The splendour falls on castle walls', one of the songs later added to *The Princess*.

April (late) He is back in London.

May

5 (Fri) He dines at Coventry Patmore's, where he meets Ralph Waldo Emerson and others, including Brookfield. Emerson and T spend the evening at B's, where they meet his wife Jane and young Henry Hallam.

6 Accepting T's invitation, Emerson calls on T at his lodgings near Buckingham Gate. A young clergyman is present, and E is denied the opportunity for the conversation he anticipated. (He leaves on Monday for Paris, and returns a month later to find T has left London.)

17 From London T writes to Mrs Burton at Somersby rectory, telling her he has sent his godson a silver cup which he had meant to send months ago.

29 He reaches Exeter for a tour in Cornwall, principally to places associated with King Arthur.

30 He reaches Bude in the dark, and soon falls over a wall on his way to the sea.

June

1 (Thurs) Calls in a doctor, to attend to his knee.

2 The doctor, after hearing T make many inquiries about him, takes him to his brother-in-law Robert Stephen Hawker, poet and vicar of Morwenstow, to whom he appears like 'a tall swarthy Spanish-looking man'. T tells him he wishes to write a poem on Arthur, some of it with Lyonnesse as its background.

4 In wet unpleasant weather T sits amid the ruins of Tintagel Castle, the cliff looking weird, 'all black and red and yellow'.

7 He finds King Arthur's stone at Slaughter Bridge near Camelford.

9 At Fowey he sends for the doctor (he is 'laid up' till the 12th with knee trouble).

14 He is still in bed. The geologist Mr Peach calls. T reads part of *Oedipus Coloneus*.

17 'Mr Peach showed me zoophytes, corallines, a spider, strange sights through microscope.'
20 T sets off for Polperro. 'Turf-fires on the hills; jewel-fires in the waves from the oar which the Cornish call "bryming".'
21 He goes to Lostwithiel, inspects the palace remains, and visits Restormel Castle, with its great circular keep muffled in ivy.
30 He travels to Truro by coach.

July
4 (Tues) Reaches Penzance, after entering with candles into a great cave. A Mr S—— had carried him on his back through the surf.
6 T goes past the Logan Rock to Land's End.
7 Visits St Michael's Mount and dines there with Edward St Aubyn.
10 From the Lizard he makes his way via Pentreath beach to Kynance Cove and into caves on Asparagus Island; sits watching wave-rainbows. He watches the sunset from Lizard Point.
27 Reaches home (Cheltenham) after visiting St Ives, Truro, Falmouth, Plymouth (from which he goes to Mount Edgcumbe, Tavistock, Morwell Rocks, and up to Dartmoor), and Exeter.

September (early) T is again having treatment at Dr Gully's, Malvern.

9 September He informs Moxon that he will be with Dr Gully a few weeks, and refers to Forster's pique at not having had an acknowledgment from him (T) for his review of *The Princess* in *The Examiner* (8 Jan 1848). Moxon is invited to come for a few days. 'Here are splendid hills and the finest air in England.'

4 November Fitz reports that T is in London, 'just emerged from the water-process at Malvern. He now drinks a bottle of wine a day, and smokes as before; a sure way to throw back in a week or two all the benefit (if benefit there were) which resulted from many weeks of privation and penance.'

11 November T, after apparently leaving two days ago for Florence with his brother Frederick, re-appears at noon in Fitz's rooms (19 Charlotte Street, Rathbone Place, London), and stays for hours until 'packed off' to dine with a friend.

November (late) T, now residing at 25 Mornington Place, Hampstead, has gone to a new doctor. Fitz regrets that he thinks more about his bowels and nerves than about 'the Laureate wreath he was born to inherit'.

December He sees much of T, who lives not far away and is still as 'noble and droll' as he used to be.

1849

14 January In London, T has been invited to dinner by Lord Monteagle, but he does not mean to dine out if he can avoid so doing.

22 January 'More full than ever of King Arthur', he calls on Aubrey de Vere at Mortlake. He promises to print his elegies (on AH) and let a few of his friends have copies.

28 February At Bonchurch on the Isle of Wight, he cannot find his 'book of elegies', a 'long butcher-ledger-like book', and believes he left it in his 'old chambers'. He asks Coventry Patmore to see if he can secure it; T expects to see him late the next evening at Mornington Place. (The book is retrieved.)

March

23 (Fri) The sculptor Thomas Woolner, who wishes to do a portrait of T, calls too late in the evening, he being about to leave London for Kent.

24 T's 'To ——, after Reading a Life and Letters', a poem which expresses his detestation of prying biographers, appears in *The Examiner*.

29 He is back at 25 Mornington Place near Hampstead Road.

31 Through the kindness of Harry Hallam, F. T. Palgrave is asked to meet T at the house of Hallam's cousin by marriage,

W. H. Brookfield, in Portman Street. T and P walk towards Hampstead, discussing universities and *The Princess*.

2 April Palgrave visits T, who reads him the songs he intends to insert in *The Princess*, and 'poems on A. Hallam, some exquisite'.

April T writes on a Sunday from Cheltenham to Mary Howitt, regretting that he cannot come and meet Mrs Gaskell, 'authoress of that fine book Mary Barton'.

June At Park House he meets Edward Lear for the first time.

16 July Writing a business letter, T gives as his address 'Carstairs, Scotland', probably anticipating a projected visit (see below).

September It is generally assumed that his Scottish tour begins in September, T staying first with Francis Garden and his wife in Edinburgh, then moving on to Carstairs. On the 4th Frederick Pollock pays 'a flying visit' there, and finds T with Milnes and the Gardens. What course he follows afterwards is not clear. He enjoys a splendid voyage from Oban to Skye, delights in Inverary, but enjoys no day more than the one he spends visiting the monument of Burns at Kirk Alloway and the banks of 'bonny Doon'. He is driven from Millport on the island of Great Cumbrae in the Clyde estuary by an outbreak of cholera, and travels with a companion (to whom he does not reveal his identity until they part) as he approaches the Highlands, in first a coach and then a gig, from Dunkeld to Pitlochry and the Pass of Killiecrankie.

2 October He has been at Cheltenham only a short time, and expects to set off for Lincolnshire in a day or two. (During the month a favourable review by Aubrey de Vere of T's *Poems* and *The Princess* appears in *The Edinburgh Review*.)

October (late) T is at Skegness; he has stayed at Halton Holgate with Charles and Elizabeth Mundy.

November He has moved to Mablethorpe, after receiving at Scremby Hall (Lincolnshire) a letter from John Forster, with an extract from one by Mrs Gaskell, indicating the enthusiasm of an old Lancashire handloom weaver, Samuel Bamford, for T's poetry, and wondering whether he dare ask T to give Bamford a volume of his poems and autograph it on the title-page. (T obliges, reckoning Bamford's admiration 'the highest honour' he has received.)

18 (Sun) He dines at the Rawnsleys', Halton Holgate. Sophy is present with her husband, Mr Elmhirst. Weston Cracroft, who had grown up at Harrington Hall, observes T critically, and Mrs R quietly rebukes him for putting his feet up on the sofa.

19 T visits Edward Rawnsley at Raithby Hall.

23 He returns to London.

24 He sends alternative versions of his song 'Sweet and low' to Emily Sellwood, asking her to say which she prefers for inclusion in *The Princess*.

27 T dines at Forster's, and meets Brookfield, Macready, and Thackeray.

December

7 (Fri) He has taken rooms in Lincoln's Inn Fields (near Forster).

10 He writes to Drummond Rawnsley (T. H. Rawnsley's second son), vicar of Shiplake-on-Thames, asking him if he may visit him next Monday or during Christmas week. (His visit to Emily Sellwood at Hale Place near Farnham may have already taken place.)

25 He tells Drummond's wife (formerly Catherine Franklin) that he is to be married in a month. This is a secret; he does not mean even his family to know.

1850

January (?) T thanks Miss Hollway (of Spilsby) for her kind note, and for a copy of her cousin Jean Ingelow's book of poems, *A Rhyming Chronicle*. (Jean was born at Boston, Lincolnshire, in 1820).

17 January He has left London for Leicestershire, where he stays at Shawell with Sophy Elmhirst and her husband, the rector.

February (mid) He has returned to Shawell, after the appearance of a new edition of *The Princess* with its intercalary songs, emphasizing the importance of the child theme. He tells Aubrey de Vere he has not worked on the elegies recently, but expects to print about twenty-five copies, which will be sent to friends on condition that they are returned or burned.

March (early) He meets Fitz in London, and asks Moxon to print six copies of the elegies. 'Give none away and retain none yourself', he adds.

1 April Emily Sellwood (as T had wished) has seen the copy sent to the Rawnsleys at Shiplake; she has read the poems 'through and through and through' with 'admiration and delight, not unmixed with awe'. They include the prologue (added in 1849), which may have given her welcome reassurance on his Christian faith.

23 April William Wordsworth, the Poet Laureate, dies. (A few days later T informs Forster that, if he and Leigh Hunt are the contenders for the Laureateship, as *The Spectator* suggests, he hopes it will fall to Hunt.)

21 May T, who hates London in the summer, is at Park House.

May (late) *In Memoriam A. H. H.* is published anonymously. Its title had been supplied by Emily Sellwood. By this time, thanks largely to Charles Turner, who, as soon as he was convinced that his brother had made up his mind, had seen the Sellwoods, and brought Emily and T together at Shiplake, T's marriage is agreed upon; Emily, fearful of the responsibility, had been encouraged by Charles Kingsley. Henry Sellwood could no longer oppose it: Emily's love had never really died; Louisa and Charles, who had been happily reunited in 1849, were much in favour of it; and T, with much improved prospects of financial security, and no longer a victim of epileptic fears, needed only to be more decisive. (The marriage licence, which made the proclamation of banns unnecessary, was dated 15 May.)

June

1 (Sat) *The Publishers' Circular* announces T as the author of *In Memoriam*.

13 T and Emily are married at Shiplake-on-Thames. (He had written suddenly to Catherine Rawnsley, telling her that 'the shirts may be gone on with'. She had little time to prepare the cake, the bride's wedding-dress, and T's 'essential

wedding garments'. 'Neither the cake nor the dresses arrived in time, and the white gloves were lost, but the wedding notwithstanding took place.' The only family representatives were Cecilia and Edmund Lushington, Henry Sellwood and Charles Weld, husband of Emily's sister Anne.)

14 T and Emily write from Pangbourne (near Reading) to thank Catherine Rawnsley; they will probably move on to 'somewhere near Weston upon Mare if not there'. T writes to Sophy Elmhirst: 'We seem to get on very well together. I have not beaten her yet.'

(In accordance with Emily's wish – 'It seemed a kind of consecration to go there' – they proceed to Clevedon, to see AH's burial-place, and are guests of his uncle Sir Charles Elton at Clevedon Court. They travel on via Lynton, Glastonbury, Clifton, and Bath, to Cheltenham, to see T's mother and 'the rest of the family living there'.)

22 George Henry Lewes, in *The Leader*, expects *In Memoriam* to become 'the solace and delight of every house where poetry is loved', and thinks T the 'greatest living poet'.

17 July From Cheltenham T requests Moxon to send a *handsomely* bound copy of *In Memoriam* to his aunt Mrs Russell of 17 Lansdowne Place, Cheltenham, and another to his father-in-law (now at the vicarage, Grasby, with Louisa and Charles). (About this time, or a little later in July, a second impression of *In Memoriam* appears. A third follows at the end of August; with the fourth, to which section lix has been added, 8000 copies have been printed by Jan 1851.)

21 July T and Emily are staying at a hotel overlooking Ullswater, at Patterdale. In a day or two they will proceed to Tent Lodge, Coniston Water, which Mrs James Garth Marshall (Lord Monteagle's daughter, sister of Stephen Spring Rice) has offered 'for as long as we choose to stay', T writes to Sophy Elmhirst.

July (end) Spedding, discovering they are at a Keswick hotel, induces them to stay with him at Mirehouse, Bassenthwaite. They have discovered a Marshall residence by almost every lake they have seen, belonging to several brothers who have inherited or bought estates and are all as rich as Croesus. They reach Tent Lodge probably on the 31st.

August

2 (Fri) They have sent for the complimentary copy of Wordsworth's *The Prelude* (published 20 July by Moxon) which has been forwarded to Cheltenham.

12 (probably) Coventry Patmore comes at T's invitation to Tent Lodge. He reports that Mrs T, without being brilliant or literary, has 'instruction and intellect enough to make the stock-in-trade of half-a-dozen literary ladies', and that she 'waits upon [T] and attends to him as she ought to do'.

14 He gives T a copy of William Allingham's *Poems* (1850), and admits his jealousy of T's admiration of them.

Before leaving, the Ts are visited by Carlyle, Venables and Aubrey de Vere (Mrs Marshall's cousin), Woolner (who models a medallion of T – not the well-known one, which was made in 1856), Franklin Lushington, Edward Lear, and Matthew Arnold. De Vere realizes Mrs T's desire to make T more religious; she has 'a great distaste for "High Church" opinions and a great horror of Rome', for which reason he keeps off such subjects. During this period T composes new passages on the prince's 'weird' seizures for the 1851 edition of *The Princess*.

October

14 (Mon) T and Emily leave Coniston for Cheltenham, travelling with Matthew Arnold as far as Crewe.

23 They reach Park House.

25 T asks Moxon to send Charles Weld (a secretary of the Royal Society) two copies of *In Memoriam*. AH's brother Henry (called to the bar in May) dies of fever at Siena, only just twenty-six years of age. About this time T writes to Derwent Coleridge, telling him he had met his brother Hartley one night at the Salutation Inn, Ambleside; he was 'full of humour and of kindliness with a flow of eloquence, which must I think have somewhat resembled his father's'.

5 November Queen Victoria offers T the Poet Laureateship, after it had been declined by Samuel Rogers. (On being assured that no birthday ode would be required of him, T accepts on the 13th. The official appointment was made on the 19th.)

November (mid) At Park House, Milnes is their guest for a few days. They are looking for a house at £60 p.a. Inquiries have been made in the Cheltenham area, and the Elmhirsts in Leicestershire and the Rawnsleys in Lincolnshire have been asked to let them know if there are any suitable places near them. Mrs Marshall has offered Tent Lodge; Milnes, a wing of Fryston Hall; and Lady Ashburton, a house near Croydon.

December (early) T sends Drummond Rawnsley his poem 'To the Vicar of Shiplake', four verses of which were composed on his wedding-day.

15 December T visits Charles Weld's office, and autographs the copy of *In Memoriam* he had recently given his assistant Walter White.

28 December The Ts at Park House are still looking for a house. The year has brought wonderful changes in the poet's fortune, and G. H. Lewes's forecast on *In Memoriam* is well on the way to fulfilment.

1851

January

18 (?) (Sat) After T has looked for a house in Twickenham, and he and Emily have stayed briefly at hotels in Cuckfield and Horsham in Sussex, they enter their first home, an old secluded house at Warninglid (in the same region), commanding a fine view of the South Downs.

19 (?) A gale springs up in the afternoon, and part of their bedroom wall is blown down during the night.

20 They decide to move; before doing so, T writes the last of the 'weird seizures' for *The Princess*.

21 He sets off to look for a house at Twickenham.

22 Having seen one to let which needs considerable repairs, he wishes he had found time to look at Chapel House during his previous visit. It is in excellent order, has high rooms and a splendid staircase, and commands beautiful views from the upper windows. In the meantime it has been let, it seems.

February

2 (Sun) The Ts leave Warninglid to stay with the Rawnsleys

at Shiplake, Emily being wheeled the first two miles by T because of her pregnancy.

3 They reach Shiplake vicarage, where they meet T. H. Rawnsley. (Later Charles Kingsley comes over from Eversley, and the search for a house continues. They begin reading Kingsley's *Alton Locke*.)

18 They set off for Park House (which they reach on the 20th), the journey being halted at the Clarendon Hotel, Reigate, where ET falls down a step, strains her side, and is in such pain that she has to keep to her bed some time.

22 T's annoyance that he could not accept Sophy Elmhirst's invitation to stay with her because of the removal to Warninglid has been misunderstood, and he writes to explain and reassure her that he remains hers affectionately.

24 In London the Ts drive about in search of appropriate dress for his presentation to the Queen. (They are still reading *Alton Locke* about this time.)

26 As he has not obtained a court dress, T is unable to attend the Queen's *levée*. (Hearing this, Rogers offers to lend his – worn by Wordsworth in 1845 – and T accepts it, though it is a tight fit. With Henry Taylor he has looked at the two houses in Twickenham which are to let, one being Chapel House, which he soon agrees to rent.)

March

3 (Mon) While staying with Sir Alexander Duff Gordon, he attends an evening party given by Lord John Russell, at which he is introduced to Baron Bunsen and the Duke of Argyll.

5 T dines with the James Marshalls of Tent Lodge.

6 He is presented to the Queen by Lord Monteagle.

7 With Thackeray, Dickens, and Forster, he is one of the stewards and many guests at the grand banquet marking the retirement of the actor Macready. Forster, proposing a toast to dramatic literature, reads the Poet Laureate's sonnet 'To W. C. Macready', which had been published in *The Times* on the 3rd.

10 The Ts leave Park House for Twickenham, sleeping at Rochester.

11 At Chapel House they dine with Spedding and Coventry Patmore to celebrate their removal. (Later visitors include

James Marshall, Henry Taylor, Charles and Louisa Turner, and Emily's father.)

During the month T writes 'To the Queen'; it appears as the dedication of *Poems*, 7th edition, 1851.

20 April (Easter Sunday) The Ts' baby, a sturdy-looking boy, dies strangled in the course of birth (as a result of Emily's fall, the doctor said).

7 May T writes to Lord Monteagle and Samuel Rogers, and explains that he is not well enough to attend the Queen's Ball. He intends to go on the 19th.

June

7 (Sat) The Ts are at Cheltenham.

17 Henry Hallam drives with his daughter Julia to Twickenham, and finds Alfred and Emily weeding the garden.

28 The Irish poet William Allingham calls at Chapel House, and notices T's slight stoop, short-sightedness, loose dark hair and beard, hollow cheeks and unhealthy pallor, and the carelessness of his attire; T is suffering from hay-fever. Mrs T is sweet and courteous; she persuades WA to stay for dinner. In his study, overlooking gardens and trees at the back, T discusses some of WA's *Poems*, then some of George Meredith's, giving particular praise to 'Love in the Valley' (its author only twenty-three). Coventry Patmore arrives, and they discuss 'grave matters' over port. T's faith rests on his belief in Intelligence and Immortality.

Late June or early July The Ts visit the Great Exhibition at the Crystal Palace in Hyde Park, and are delighted with the building and the great glass fountain.

15 July They leave for Boulogne on their way to Italy.

20 July They are in Paris with Edmund and Cecilia Lushington; in the Louvre T has been recognised by Robert and Elizabeth Browning (*née* Barrett). (On their way from Florence to London, they are invited to tea by the Ts, whom they meet several times; he offers them accommodation and servants at Chapel House.)

12 August After visiting the Italian Riviera and Genoa, the Ts reach Bagni di Lucca (recommended by RB) in the evening. (Later they are astonished to see Richard Jesse, Emily's husband, who has heard of their arrival. During their three weeks' stay they spend time with Francis Garden and his wife.)

September (early) They leave for Florence (where they stay with Frederick T and his wife at the Villa Torregiani. Mrs Trollope, authoress and mother of the novelist Anthony Trollope, calls on them.)

24 September They leave Florence for Paris, travelling via Milan, Como, and the 'snowy Splügen' Pass into Switzerland. (In Paris the Brownings, on their return journey to Florence, call on them affectionately.)

October The Ts return to Twickenham.

November Another 5000 copies of *In Memoriam* are printed.

4 December Emily T acknowledges the drawings of Italian landscapes which Edward Lear has sent as a wedding-present.

27 December Fitz brings his friend Edward Cowell, the Persian scholar, and his wife to dine with the Ts at Chapel House. (ET and Mrs Cowell become devoted friends.)

1852

January

12 (Mon) T is at Cheltenham to see his mother and his sister Mary Ker (married in July 1851) before she leaves for Antigua. (He remains there until the 26th, his literary efforts concentrated on poems, to be published anonymously in the press, urging England to prepare for defence against the French, after Louis Napoleon's December *coup d'état*.)

24 'The Penny-Wise' appears in *The Morning Chronicle*.

28 ET writes from Chapel House to Patmore on the distribution of notices he has sent for organizing a volunteer rifle corps. She encloses a copy of 'Rifle Clubs!!!'

31 T's 'Britons, Guard Your Own' appears anonymously in John Forster's *The Examiner*.

7 February 'The Third of February' (marking the day when the House of Lords rejected the bill for the reorganization of the Militia) and 'Hands All Round!' (signed 'Merlin') are published in *The Examiner*.

8 February In a letter to Brookfield, Franklin Lushington remarks on T's stupidity in not staying in Italy for the winter; his chief reason for returning had been 'the want of English tobacco'.

26 March After calling at Cheltenham, the Ts begin their stay with John Rashdall (one of T's college friends) at Great Malvern vicarage; they spend much time looking in vain for a country residence.

May (late) They stay about two weeks at Cheltenham, where they bid farewell to Mary (who had suddenly announced her marriage to Alan Ker, an unsuccessful local barrister with whom she is setting out for Antigua).

16 June They return to Twickenham with Matilda T. (T visits the Exhibition in London with his sister, and is delighted with Millais's *Ophelia* and *The Huguenot*, the latter especially. Henry Taylor introduces them to the Camerons, who live near, at Sheen Lodge, East Sheen.)

25 June ET writes to Mrs Cameron, telling her she must not sacrifice her time to find a house for her and T. (Both have been reluctant to stay at Chapel House since the death of their first-born; and mists, damp, bad drains, and the smell of local cabbage patches, have increased T's distaste for the place.)

July Early this month Franklin Lushington, the Coventry Patmores, and Woolner (soon to leave for Australia, hoping to make a fortune in gold-digging) dine with the Ts.

7 (Wed) T travels to London for York, where he witnesses electioneering drunkenness, and mob brawling and violence.

8 He reaches Whitby, hoping the sea air will rid him of hay-fever.
20 He goes to Scarborough by the packet-boat.
21 Visiting Grasby, he walks through the fields and admires the wheat. It is 'a nice little place they have' (the new vicarage, where Charles and Louisa are probably now in residence).
27 He is going to stay tomorrow to see the school-feast, children in sack-races and doing 'all manner of queer things' (almost certainly in the field directly below the new vicarage).
31 After seeing the new dock at Grimsby (a development which was to add considerable value to Frederick's estate), he is at Louth, on his way to Crowland Abbey.

August
Early this month T is back at Twickenham, where Emily has had the company of Matilda, then of her own sister Anne with her husband Charles Weld.
9 (Mon) Writing to thank F. W. Farrar for the copy of his Chancellor's Medal prize-winning poem, he says he could wish his own ('Timbuctoo') had never been written.
11 Hallam T is born prematurely, two days after ET had sent an invitation to the Brownings for the 13th.
16 T invites Henry Hallam to be his son's godfather.

September (early) He makes a short visit to the Isle of Wight, where he sees his friend James White at Bonchurch.

14 September The Duke of Wellington dies (and T soon begins to feel that he will be expected to write on the event).

5 October Hallam is christened, Henry Hallam, F. D. Maurice, and Mrs Marshall acting as sponsors. Other guests include Charles and Louisa, the Welds, Matilda, Drummond Rawnsley, Browning (his wife not being allowed to come because of the cold wind), Palgrave, Edmund Lushington, Venables, the Brookfields, Aubrey de Vere, Henry Taylor, and the Camerons.

October (end) The Ts leave Chapel House, floods and colds adding to their dissatisfaction with the place. They move to Seaford House (at Seaford, on the south coast between Brighton and Eastbourne, and not far from the South Downs and Beachy

Head). T rents it for a short period, lasting into the New Year.

November

16 (Tues) T's 'Ode on the Death of the Duke of Wellington' is published. 10,000 copies are printed, to be sold at one shilling a copy.

18 T witnesses the Duke's funeral procession, but not the burial service in St Paul's Cathedral. His ode is sold in large numbers to spectators in the streets.

23 From Seaford House he thanks Henry Taylor for his appreciation of the Wellington ode.

8 December T informs Moxon he will return part of the £200 paid for the ode if he (the publisher) is out of pocket.

27–8 December Fitz visits the Ts at Seaford. T has altered and enlarged his ode quite successfully, he thinks, but is disappointed with its reception.

1853

January (early) Arthur Hugh Clough spends a few days in Sussex (at Seaford presumably) with T, for the sake of his health.

17 January In London T goes with Fitz to hear the first part of the Wellington ode sung to the music of the Lincolnshire composer George French Flowers. Fitz finds the music dull.

11 February The Ts have just returned to Twickenham from Brighton. (In Jan 1870 Fitz remembered Brighton in 1853 'when you and Mrs Tennyson were there, and I with my Mother'.)

1 March T declines to stand for the Rectorship of Edinburgh University. (Later he changes his mind, but is relieved when he is not elected.)

6 April He attends a meeting of the Cosmopolitan Club; Milnes and Spedding are present. (In the latter part of the month he and

Emily are at Farnham, looking for a house. Charles Kingsley, as vivacious as ever, comes over from Eversley to see them.)

May (early) Still at Farnham, T writes to Emily on a refusal a lawyer had given him of Elstead Lodge; he has found time to walk over to Hale Place (where she had lived with her father from 1848 until her marriage).

11 May They have been at Park House more than a week.

July (second half) They travel to York (where Palgrave joins them), Whitby, Redcar, and Richmond. ET, who is suffering from the effects of pregnancy, goes with Hallam T to stay with the Turners at Grasby, while T sets off with Palgrave for Scotland.

27 July They reach Edinburgh.

29 July Palgrave, feeling that T is indifferent towards him, stays while T visits the Monteiths at Carstairs.

August

3 (Wed) From Oban T visits Iona and Staffa with Palgrave and the latter's old Balliol friend, the classical scholar William Sellar.

6 They are staying at Ardtornish, Sellar's home on the isle of Morvern.

13 T is in Edinburgh, hoping to tour Sutherland with Sellar. (He remains there until about the end of the month after two unexpected surgical operations. During this period he writes 'The Daisy', on finding the flower he picked for Emily as they were travelling up the Splügen Pass pressed in the book she had lent him.)

September (early) Perhaps it is at this time that he visits Cecilia and Edmund in Glasgow, before renewing the search for a house in England.

October After the Ts have returned to Twickenham, T again visits James White and Edmund Peel on the Isle of Wight. He is still hoping to find a suitable house, and, hearing that Farringford is to let, he visits it. It looks 'rather wretched' and neglected, but it is secluded and has the kind of accommodation he is looking for, with excellent opportunities for the privacy of neighbouring walks or, within easy range, along high cliffs above the sea at the top of chalk downland stretching west to the Needles. The view it affords from the front across to Freshwater Bay and beyond, with St Catherine's Hill in the distance, can only please. Farringford has so much to offer, T feels he must consult Emily on the question of renting it without delay. He may already have thought of further developing 'Oh! that 'twere possible', for her father sends ET a copy from *The Tribute* at her request.

November

1 (?) (Tues) William Allingham (who gives 'Thursday the first of November') travels by train from London to Richmond to see T at Chapel House. T asks him to stay and dine, gives him a book, and brings Hallam down in his arms. In the drawing-room WA finds Frederick T and Fitz. The men smoke and tell stories, 'some of an ammoniacal saltness', in T's study.

Soon after this T and Emily travel by train to Brockenhurst in the New Forest, and on by coach to Lymington, whence they are rowed over in the evening to the Isle of Wight. ET observes a dark heron flying over the Solent against the 'daffodil sky'. When, next day, from the Farringford drawing-room, she looks at the park-like foreground, the blue of Freshwater Bay, the down on the left, and rosy capes beyond, she knows she 'must have that view'.

11 T accepts a three-year lease of Farringford, with the option of purchase at the end of the period. The rent is £2 a week, furnished.

14 He writes to Moxon for an advance of £1000, £400 of which is owed to him. He proposes investing in East Lincolnshire Railway Stock, and estimates that, with income from his poetry, he will manage. (His income – very high for a poet – is much greater than he cares to admit, as it has been for years.)

24 They leave Chapel House, and stay the night at Lymington.

25 They begin life at Farringford. Soon two of their maids are in tears, not wishing to live in such a remote place.

(T arranges with his mother, Matilda, and his brothers at Cheltenham, that they shall take over his remaining lease, and live, at Twickenham.)

1854

January The year opens with the booming of cannon at Portsmouth, the artillery practising for war against Russia in the Crimea. T writes the poem 'To the Rev. F. D. Maurice', inviting him to Farringford after dismissal from his professorship at King's College, London.

28 February His hopes of being able to purchase Farringford are raised by Moxon's plans (first proposed on 11 Jan) to publish an illustrated edition of his poems.

16 March ET gives birth to another son. (He is named Lionel because, when he hears the news, T is observing the culmination of Mars in the sign of the Lion.)

29 March T informs Forster that he has an affliction of his right eye, caused by trying to read some Persian text. He has been correcting proofs of his brother Frederick's poems *Days and Hours*.

April He takes Emily out in her garden chair to see the 'wealth of Daffodils' and the ruby sheaths of the lime trees. (She has been unable to walk for a month after Lionel's birth.)

May

15 (Mon) T Travels to London with Edmund Lushington and Coventry Patmore.

18 T is staying at 60 Lincoln's Inn Fields. He calls at Moxon's to discuss the proposed illustrated edition of his poems, then visits a number of artists, including John Millais, who agrees to come to Farringford and sketch Hallam for an illustration of 'Dora'.

19 He goes to the new Crystal Palace at Sydenham with Charles Weld, and does not think it worth while to see the opening of the exhibition, as it will not be as impressive as the

last, in 1851. Afterwards he and Horatio T dine with Franklin Lushington at the Oxford and Cambridge Club. Tom Taylor comes to Spedding's in the evening, and gives T a book of Breton ballads.

20 T dines with JS, Pollock, and the two painters Daniel Maclise and William Boxall, at Forster's.

23 T returns to Farringford.

25 Fitz arrives at Farringford (and stays for two weeks, during which he plays Mozart and Handel on ET's piano, and works at Persian with T, who has already begun *Maud*, which he reads to Fitz).

6 June Lionel is baptized, Franklin Lushington acting as one godfather, Fitz as proxy for the other, Drummond Rawnsley. Sir John Simeon arrives as the christening-party comes home from the church. (It is his first visit to Farringford; he is a Catholic but becomes one of T's greatest friends. Subsequently he helps in the development of *Maud* when T is at a standstill, suggesting that he work backwards from the lyric 'Oh! that 'twere possible', from which it began, to create in effect a more narrative subject. His garden and trees at Swainston Hall combine with the Farringford setting – including the sea – to provide the main background of the poem. The socio-economic criticism which it voices owes much to the views of Carlyle, Kingsley, and Maurice.)

7 June T writes to George Grove (the music historian), secretary of the Crystal Palace Company, thanking him for the invitation, and regretting that he and his wife are unable to attend the opening of the Crystal Palace on the 10th. (Grove had wished him to write an ode for the occasion.)

August

11 (Fri) Hallam T is taken to Alum Bay for his birthday; he enjoys driving a donkey, and is taken by boat to Scratchell's Bay.

12 T leaves for a holiday tour (which takes him first to Glastonbury, Yeovil, and caves at Cheddar).

17 He visits Corfe Castle, Christchurch, and Bournemouth.

21 He returns to Farringford.

September T continues *Maud*. After being the guest of his friend

Sir John Simeon at Swainston Hall, Aubrey de Vere stays at Farringford. He finds T 'much happier and proportionately less morbid than he used to be', and thinks nobly of ET (who had been on her guard, knowing he had recently been converted to Catholicism); she is 'full of soul as well as mind'. He and T have several breezy walks on the downs, sometimes to the Needles. They agree in 'greatly admiring' Coventry Patmore's recently published poem, the first part ('The Betrothal') of *The Angel in the House*.

23 October T informs F. J. Furnivall, a teacher at the Working Men's College in Red Lion Square, that he is requesting Moxon to send him as many of his books as he requires for the college.

30 October T gratefully acknowledges the gift of *The Angel in the House: The Betrothal* from its author.

November

1 (Wed) Moxon arrives, and discusses the publication of T's poems.

14 T receives an account of the charge of the Heavy Brigade at Balaclava containing the sentence 'Our ears were frenzied by the monotonous incessant cannonade going on for days together.' (The poem he wrote on the subject was not begun until 1881, when he had learnt much more on this audacious event.)

22 John Millais comes, and stays for three days, during which he sketches Hallam T and ET.

December (early) T writes 'The Charge of the Light Brigade' after reading of 'a hideous blunder' (which he remembered as 'someone had blundered') at Balaclava in *The Times*. The next day ET sends it to John Forster for publication in *The Examiner*, where it appears on the 9th.

December (late) F. T. Palgrave and his brother are staying at a hotel on the Isle of Wight. Both visit Farringford several times, as P does at this season in succeeding years until 1863.

1855

January News from the Crimea is still depressing, indicative of incapacity and neglect.

February

1 (Thurs) Arctic weather has set in, waves freezing on the shore of Freshwater Bay. ET notes 'the snow folding in and out of the hedge like drapery'.

5 Woolner, a favourite with ET (and later with her boys), is at Farringford, where he begins working on a plaster medallion of T, not being satisfied with the one he made (in 1851) before going to Australia. (He leaves on the 19th.)

8 ET acknowledges the volumes of Poe which F. G. Tuckerman, an American poet who had visited him in January, has sent T.

21 March John Ruskin writes, inviting T to see his Turner paintings; he has discovered Alfred's interest from Woolner.

8 April T stays another day at Bonchurch in order to see double stars through Dr Mann's telescope.

25 April The Ts return home from Swainston, where T reads *Maud*. He finishes copying it up for publication.

May The Ts visit London, and take their children to the Crystal Palace. They meet Ruskin, and Lady Franklin and Sophy Cracroft.

7 June T thanks Lear for sending a copy of his *Book of Nonsense* (1846), which Hallam will enjoy.

20 June After taking the children and their nurse to Park House, T and Emily are at Oxford, guests of Robert Scott, Master of Balliol. He receives the honorary degree of Doctor of Civil Law, an award proposed by Frederick Temple (later Archbishop of Canterbury, now Principal of Kneller Hall, a training-college for teachers – not far from Chapel House, Twickenham – where Palgrave is Vice-Principal) and actively supported by Benjamin Jowett of Balliol. Though nervous when he enters the Sheldonian for the presentation, he is not disconcerted by the wag who finds an allusion to 'The May Queen' irresistible, and calls out, 'Did your mother call you early, dear?' He receives his degree with two others, both successful British commanders in the Crimea. There are shouts for *In Memoriam* and the battles of Alma and Inkerman, and T is pleased to think that he receives 'the larger share' of the undergraduates' applause. Afterwards, wearing his red doctoral robes, he smokes in the Master of Balliol's walled-in garden. In the evening he talks with Gladstone and Montalembert at Magdalen. (The next day he and Emily view Raphael sketches in the Ashmolean, and illuminated missals in the Bodleian. After tea they look through the big telescope at the nebulae in Cassiopeia, the ring nebula in Lyra, and some double stars.)

7 July They return to Farringford, and *Maud* is given 'the last touch' before being sent to Moxon.

28 July *Maud, and Other Poems* is published. The volume includes the Wellington ode, 'The Charge of the Light Brigade', 'The Daisy', and 'The Brook'.

August

6 (Mon) In response to a suggestion which has come indirectly from a chaplain in the Crimea, T initiates the printing of 1000 copies of 'The Charge of the Light Brigade' for distribution among the soldiers on the Sebastopol front. (Another 1000 are sent later.) T begins his lasting friendship with Granville Bradley, a master at Rugby (afterwards Headmaster of Marlborough, Master of University College, Oxford, and Dean of Westminster), who is on holiday at Alum Bay, not far from Farringford.

14 The news of Henry Lushington's death reaches the Ts, causing great distress.(After AH, he was T's dearest friend. News of his illness made Venables set off to bring him home; he died on the 11th while they were in Paris.)

25 T receives from Bradley a copy of Matthew Arnold's *Poems* (1855).

31 After leaving for the Peak on the 29th, T is on his way by gig to Lyndhurst.

(Many readers having failed to appreciate the dramatic qualities of *Maud*, thinking the mad hero ventriloquizes throughout T's disapproval of England, T, though oversensitive and self-centred in his responses, has reason to be taken aback by the hostility which his poem engenders, especially among reviewers.)

September

1 (Sat) T loses his way in the New Forest, where he seeks impressions for 'Merlin and Vivien'.

3 He returns, after enjoying his week at Salisbury and in the New Forest near Lyndhurst.

4 Frederick Pollock and his wife visit Farringford.T reads part of *Maud*, and they are taken to see Hallam and Lionel asleep in bed before leaving. (The next day the remainder of *Maud* is read to them in the garden before dinner.)

17 Palgrave leaves after staying about ten days at Farringford.

25 T leaves to visit his dentist in London (where he stays until 2 Oct).

27 He is at the Brownings', very grateful to Robert, who has read *Maud* four times and (a master of the dramatic lyric himself) declared it a great poem. After dinner William and Dante Gabriel Rossetti arrive, and T becomes plaintively obsessed with the injustices of his critics. Mrs B rescues him by asking him to read *Maud*, and D. G. Rossetti sketches him as he intones.

30 He dines with the Camerons.

October On the 1st he is at Twickenham with his mother. In *The Westminster Review* the future George Eliot criticizes the morbidity of T's poem, and its faith in war as 'the unique social regenerator'. Patmore in *The Edinburgh Review* insists that it is not necessary to play a demagogue's role in order to traject a criticism of contemporary life; a poet belongs to 'the every-growing tradition of civilization', and 'no man reflects our age more truly' than T 'when he is not thinking of doing so'. Early in the month T receives from Charles Weld a copy of *The Asylum Journal of Mental Science*, in which the editor confirms the reality of the hero's madness.

17 October Edward Lear arrives at Farringford with Franklin Lushington; in the evening he sings his settings of 'Mariana', 'The Lotos-Eaters', 'O let the solid ground' (*Maud* I.xi), and 'Oh! that 'twere possible'. The Simeons are present. ET had asked Lear to bring her a copy of his setting for T's poem 'Edward Gray'.

November

3 (Sat) Goldwin Smith, writing anonymously in the first issue of *The Saturday Review*, condemns 'the glorification of war as a remedy for the canker of peace' in *Maud*. (Other reviewers had complained of its obscurity.)
12 Ruskin writes, expressing his admiration of *Maud* throughout. He has heard of many stupid misunderstandings of it.
28 George Brimley's defence of *Maud* in *Cambridge Essays* (1855) is acknowledged gratefully by T.

December

19 (Wed) Jowett (with an invitation for T from Lady Ashburton, The Grange, Alresford, Hampshire) arrives with Alexander Grant.
27 They depart, Grant presenting a copy of G. H. Lewes's *Goethe* to T.
28 Charles Weld arrives, and reads from his 'Vacation Tour' in Brittany (published 1856).
31 T leaves to join the literary gathering at Lady Ashburton's.

1856

January

1 (Tues) At Lady Ashburton's Brookfield observes that Goldwin Smith is 'a good deal shirked by Carlyle, Tennyson and Venables on account of his having written certain reviews obnoxious to them'.
2 B takes a walk with Smith and Carlyle while T reads *Maud* to the remainder of the company.
9 T (who returned on the 8th) reads some of Eckermann's conversations with Goethe to Emily.
22 Sir John Simeon comes and takes T to Swainston.

February

1 (Fri) He is at Ventnor, star-gazing with Dr Mann.
6 T begins reading the *Odyssey* to Emily in 'his beautiful *viva voce* translations'.

7 Woolner arrives, to work on a medallion of ET and a bust of the Laureate. (He stays until 15 Mar; T has been writing 'Merlin'.)
22 A servant is sent to pack the Ts' furniture at Chapel House.

March

1 (Sat) T finishes the *Odyssey*; Emily is sorry it is over.
15 He has been looking through proofs of R. J. Mann's 'Maud Vindicated', which the author had sent with a request for any desirable emendations.
20 'Merlin' goes on grandly, ET writes.
24 Venables and Tom Taylor and his wife arrive. She plays Beethoven, and sings some of T's songs to her settings.
30 T has just completed 'Merlin', and reads it to Venables and Emily.
31 A 'grand consultation' takes place between the Ts, Venables, and Sir John Simeon on the question of the purchase of Farringford.

April

14 (Mon) Mr Seymour, the owner, accepts T's terms for its purchase. (*Maud* is selling well.)
16 The Enid story (part of *Idylls of the King*) is begun.
21 Aunt Franklin and Sophy Cracroft drive over from Cowes for dinner.
23 (St George's Day) The Ts travel with Drummond Rawnsley and Alexander Grant to Yarmouth to see the Grand Review of the fleet. ('The sight was magnificent', ET wrote.)
30 They hear from Venables that a Mr Chapman has pronounced their title to Farringford good. ET looks at the flowers in the withy hold and park, listens to the song of nightingales and other birds, watches the 'burning splendour' of St Catherine's in the sunset, and is 'glad that Farringford is ours'.

May

10 (Sat) They are at Swainston to meet the Milneses. (Richard had married Annabella Crewe, sister of Lord Crewe, in 1851.)
12 The Milneses and the Simeons lunch at Farringford.
13 Prince Albert arrives unexpectedly in the midst of removal proceedings to the Red House, in preparation for the sale of the owner's furniture, and for cleaning and redecorations, at Farringford.

15 Emily joins T and the Simeons and Milneses at Swainston.
21 Palgrave and his friend Sellar are at Farringford, where the Ts are in suspense, having been led to think the Queen would call.
27 At the Farringford sale, furniture is bought for the Ts. The Twickenham lease having expired, they have had to store their own furniture in the meantime. The need for additional pictures is evident, and ET requests Woolner in London to buy old copies of old pictures in bright frames as cheaply as possible.

10 June At last the Ts are established in their own home. T has helped to unpack and 'place the things'. (Improvements continue in the house until the 15th.)

22 June They see a large ship sail majestically past with troops from the Crimea. (During the previous week T has been reading Chaucer to Emily.)

July

1 (Tues) Emily writes to T in London. She is 'puritan enough to be sorry' that he spent Sunday morning as he says he did, and hopes he may have made a mistake over the day in his letter. 'My idea of Sunday as a day of high spiritual enjoyment thou knowest.'

(T has had to discuss publishing and financial questions with Moxon; he has made several visits to the dentist, shown some of his poems to Spedding, and met other old friends. He has probably begun visiting Little Holland House in West Kensington, home of Thoby Prinsep, formerly a distinguished member of the India Civil Service. His wife is one of the seven half-French Pattle sisters including Mrs Cameron, all rich and born in India. The Prinseps entertain lavishly, their guests – of whom the painter G. F. Watts is well-nigh permanent – being celebrities, writers and artists particularly. T soon becomes a favourite, especially among the ladies in this admiring entourage, and he becomes a frequent visitor.)

10 The Bradleys come to the Red House for their holiday.
18 With Hallam and Lionel, the Ts leave Farringford (which they have let) for a long holiday in Wales (where Emily and

T are helped by schoolmasters to read Welsh for the study of Welsh history and the *Mabinogion*, on which T is to draw considerably for his 'Enid'.

28 After having made Llangollen their centre, they move on to Bala (where he is to complete the tournament in 'Enid' and talk at length with ET on Infinity and God). The lake is 'a beautiful violet colour with white breakers'.

August

4 (Mon) They are at Dolgelly, Cader Idris 'towering with its woods over the church and the town'.

12 They are now at Barmouth (where T had stayed in 1839).

20 They drive in the rain to Harlech.

30 They move on through misty rain to Ffestiniog.

September

6 (Sat) For the steep route to Dolgelly they set off in 'a double car' with two horses.

8 T climbs Cader Idris; heavy rain spoils the view from the top.

15 After staying at Llanidloes, and travelling to Builth, with many delightful views of the Wye on the way, T leaves his family, and sets off for Brecon. (Money running low, he makes excursions alone.)

16 He visits Caerleon (near Newport), where he sits like King Arthur among the ruins.

23 After an outing to the magnificent ruins of Raglan Castle (a place where he could have stayed for a week), and staying at Caerphilly and Merthyr Tydvil, he takes a coach to Brecon, where he rejoins his family.

26 On their way home, after travelling from Gloucester, they attend afternoon service in Salisbury Cathedral.

October

1 (Wed) Mr Moxon comes. 'Very kind about advancing us money', ET writes.

13 Engravings of the Pre-Raphaelite illustrations for T's *Poems* – the 1857 edition – are being prepared. M has arranged for a plate to be engraved from Woolner's medallion of T.

15 Coventry Patmore and his wife arrive after a rough crossing in an open boat. (They stay until the 23rd, when they go to Swainston.)
17 The Cloughs, who are staying at Freshwater,come to dinner. (Another visitor during the month is Arthur Stanley, Jowett's close friend, afterwards Dean of Westminster. James Marshall suggests that the Ts stay at Tent Lodge next year.)
22 The Ts hear from Park House that Edmund and Cecilia's only son has died.

November
Having to pay for Farringford by 2 December, T is compelled early this month to sell his railway shares at a loss. He finishes 'Enid' (the first of his *Idylls of the King*, 1859; in the much enlarged 1873 edition of the *Idylls* it is divided into two parts, entitled 'The Marriage of Geraint' and 'Geraint and Enid' in 1886).
14 (Fri) T and Emily set off for Park House via London, where they stay the night, visit the dentist, and meet Edmund Lushington.
21 They return home, after meeting friends, and seeing the dentist again, in London.
27 A copy of his wife's *Aurora Leigh* arrives from Browning.

December
16 (Tues) Plumbers, glaziers, carpenters, and bricklayers arrive, to begin work at Farringford.
18 Palgrave arrives unexpectedly with lots of books, 'a welcome sight'.
25 The Ts spend their Christmas alone. Lionel is rather better.

1857

21 January Jane Welsh Carlyle replies to ET's letter of sympathy with her in her illness, and to the invitation she has received to visit the Ts with her husband. 'If that man would leave his eternal *Frederick* and come along!', or if only she had the *nerve* to come alone, she writes.

23 February The Camerons are staying on the Isle of Wight, and dine with the Ts.

11 March T reads some of *The Wisdom of Solomon* to Emily, and tells her which passages he marked when reading it to AH.

23 March They dine with the Camerons after doing their usual work in the fields. Mrs C gives ET a beautifully bound edition of Henry Taylor's poems.

April

15 (Wed) They go to St Lawrence for Horatio T's wedding the next day.

22 Arthur Stanley comes, walks on the downs with T, hears some of *Maud*, and stays for the night.

27 T visits London to see his dentist.

28 He calls on W. B. Donne, Librarian of the London Library, concerning books on King Arthur which he had sent to ET, and sees their friend Fitz there, looking 'thinnish and worn'. He is 'staying at a great House in Kensington with which I won't meddle', the latter writes about a week later, alluding to Little Holland House with disapproval of what he regards as T's social ambitions.

May

Moxon's Illustrated Edition of T's poems at last appears; 10,000 copies are printed.

8 (Fri) T, Mrs Prinsep, and Mrs Cameron dine with John Forster, who is jolly and listens admiringly to T's reading of 'Enid'.

10 Pollock dines at Little Holland House, and meets T, Spedding, Patmore, Holman Hunt, the Camerons, and others.

14 T's breakfasting-out so far has been with Henry Hallam, but he spends all this morning with the Duke and Duchess of Argyll, to whom he reads from his *Enid and Nimuë: the True and the False* (the Enid and Merlin stories), six trial copies of which have been printed and distributed recently; later they are recalled, with the exception of Palgrave's, because one of T's college friends had borrowed a copy from the publisher, and talked disparagingly of some passages.

18 He returns home with Woolner and Vernon Lushington.

June (mid?) T asks Venables to destroy his copy of *Enid and Nimuë*.

19 June Edmund and Cecilia come to Farringford for ten days. Horatio T and his wife Charlotte ('Charlie') are already there. Bayard Taylor, the American translator of *Faust*, arrives with an introduction from Thackeray, and stays for the night. The most beautiful sight in the world, he tells T, is a Norwegian forest in winter sunshine.

July

4 (Sat) Edward Lear comes (and many guests hear his singing on the 6th).

9 T makes Emily a birthday present of his first 'Guinevere' lines, the end of Arthur's farewell speech. (He is disappointed with Moxon's ambitious Illustrated Edition of his poems, and with its sales. He does not care for most of the Pre-Raphaelite designs, and is very critical of inaccuracies in detail.)

18 After two nights in London, the Ts are on their way to Grasby. (Charles drives them one afternoon to see the imitative splendours of Bayons Manor.)

22 Moxon offers T the sum he had said he would realize for him from the sales of the Illustrated Edition, viz. £2000 (which T quickly accepts).

27 From Grasby, just before leaving for Manchester, T writes to the Duchess of Argyll, hoping he will be able to come to Inverary in October.

31 At the exhibition of paintings opened in Manchester by the Queen and Prince Albert, the Ts are accompanied by Woolner and observed by the novelist Nathaniel Hawthorne, now American consul at Liverpool. Later in the day they hear Dickens read from *A Christmas Carol* in the Free Trade Hall. (The next day they leave for Coniston.)

August–September At Tent Lodge, where they are the Marshalls' guests, they have several visitors: Allingham, Woolner, Venables, Franklin Lushington, Stephen and William Spring Rice, Matthew Arnold, and Dr Whewell. T climbs Coniston Old Man with Coventry Patmore. Visits are made to Furness Abbey, Langdale Pikes and Blea Tarn, and Wastwater. Later the Ts stay at Patterdale Hall (Ullswater) with the William Marshalls.

September
18 (Fri) C. L. Dodgson ('Lewis Carroll') walks from Ambleside to obtain permission to take photographs of the Ts; T is absent.
21 He meets T.
27 He takes photographs of the Ts and Marshalls (and again the next morning).

October The Ts had hoped to visit the Monteiths, but had not given sufficient notice. Hearing that Carstairs is full, they attempt to get into touch with the Duke and Duchess of Argyll. When they arrive at Inverary Castle, they find the Duke is at Balmoral, the Duchess at Dunrobin, Sutherland. Hearing of their arrival, the Duchess charters a steamboat, and rescues them from the inn where they have chosen to stay; the Duke returns, and they are entertained in splendour at Inverary for a week. They stay at Carstairs on their return journey (14–16 Oct), then with the Marshalls of Leeds (where they are taken over the worsted and flax mills which have been the source of vast fortunes for the Marshall families). After a stop at Peterborough, they stay a week at Park House, then another week with Cecilia and Edmund Lushington at Ashburton Cottage (the Camerons' home since 1854 and until 1860, when they move to the Isle of Wight).

4 November They reach Farringford, after a visit with Mrs Cameron to the Carlyles. T reads Emily some passages from Dante. (Soon after her return ET is afflicted with an illness that weakens her, and frequently lays her low, for the rest of her life.)

December T writes 'Sea Dreams', sweeps and rolls lawns, and reads Livingstone's *Missionary Travels* and much else. Late in the month he writes two additional verses for inclusion in 'God Save the Queen', to be sung at the wedding in January of the Princess Royal and the Crown Prince Frederick William of Prussia.

1858

January
T acknowledges *Parables from Nature*, a present from the author Mrs Gatty which he says he will encourage his boys to read when they are old enough. The Indian Mutiny of 1857 had

created great disquiet in Britain. News of the death of its hero, General Sir Henry Havelock, on 24 November (announced as on the 25th), reaches England on 7 January, and soon afterwards T writes 'Havelock', which remains unpublished during his lifetime.

7 (Thurs) The Ts finish hanging 'the Somersby pictures' (which arrived a few days previously).

8 George Eliot asks her publisher John Blackwood to send a copy of her *Scenes of Clerical Life* (newly published) to T.

12 Algernon Swinburne arrives at Farringford with a fellow-student at Balliol. T invites them to return for dinner, after which he reads them *Maud* and part of 'Guinevere'. (Soon afterwards he completes 'The Parting of Arthur and Guinevere'.)

1 February He gratefully acknowledges the receipt of Frederick Locker's *London Lyrics*.

15 February T sends a message (in ET's letter), asking Woolner not to sell his bust to an American; 'he is sure to find a purchaser in England'.

15 March T presents 'Guinevere', now 'finally completed', to Emily at tea-time.

29 March Benjamin Jowett comes. (Next day he helps to wheel ET in her chair through Maiden's Croft, St George's Field, and the meadow by the farmyard, thence home by the park.)

April

6 (Mon) The physicist John Tyndall calls; he is invited to dinner, where he meets Jowett.

8 J. W. Parker, son of the publisher, comes. (A few days later, while his guest is out walking, T decorates the summer-house – which he built early in the year – in Maiden's Croft, overlooking the down to the south.)

28 The box of books promised for loan by Mr Parker arrives. T begins reading Motley's *Rise of the Dutch Republic* to Emily,

who is reminded of happy youthful days when her father read history aloud to her and her sisters.

May

10 (Mon) James White and his wife, and the publisher John Blackwood and his wife, lunch with the Ts.

15 T copies out 'The Grandmother'. After dinner he fetches Emily to enjoy the view from the upper windows: 'rich in its May beauty of golden gorse, flowering trees and yellow-green elms bathed in sunlight and green through the mist on the hills beyond the Solent a Cuyp-like landscape'.

19 He leaves to visit his dentist in London.

22 He sees the panorama of Lucknow at Robert Burford's in Leicester Square.

25 He returns late with some Cromes, which next day he and Emily hang in the ante-room.

27 John Blackwood is sending a copy of Professor Wilson's works 'as a memorial' of his Farringford visit.

June

3 (Thurs) Edward Moxon, T's publisher, dies. (Subsequently, when T is informed that he owes the firm nearly £9000 for the Illustrated Edition of his poetry, which neither he nor his representatives had commissioned, relations become strained.)

7 Woolner wishes ET could persuade T to start 'The Maid of Astolat'.

10 T is in London again, partly for dental attention.

13 He spends the afternoon at Little Holland House, and dines there. 'Half London on the lawn.'

17 W. F. Pollock dines with J. W. Parker at his rooms over his shop in the Strand, and meets T and W. G. Clark, editor of *Essays by the Late George Brimley*.

22 A. H. Clough hears T read 'Guinevere'. (T returns home the next day.)

July

2 (Fri) The painter Holman Hunt leaves Farringford.

9 The Ts leave for their holiday, first visiting Mrs T, now living with the Jesses at Rose Mount, Hampstead.

16 Mrs Prinsep persuades them to stay at Little Holland House,

where G. F. Watts is working on his 'moonlight' portrait of T (who begins 'The Fair Maid of Astolat' and meets Ruskin there).

23 After taking his family to Grasby, where ET finds her father stronger despite his recent illness, T leaves Hull for a brief visit to Norway.

August

1 (Sun) He is in Christiania (Oslo), at the consul's house, overlooking the Sound. On the way from Kristiansand, the seas have been 'magnificent', he writes.

2 He visits the Riukan Foss (which Bayard Taylor thought the loveliest waterfall in the world), and is impressed by the 'magnificent power of water' and the 'weird blue light behind the fall'.

27 After visiting the Crystal Palace with Woolner, the Ts reach home.

30 William Michael Rossetti makes his first call on T from Freshwater Gate.

22–9 September The Frederick Maurices stay at Farringford, T reading his recent poems 'Guinevere', 'The Grandmother', and 'Sea Dreams' during their visit.

4 October At Swainston T is excited when the tail of a great comet passes over Arcturus; he keeps getting up from the dining-table, and going outside to look. (Sir John Simeon's daughter Louisa – who gives July – remembered how he kept saying, 'It is a besom of destruction sweeping the sky.')

October (later) The Ts have been astonished to hear that Maclise has been in Italy making sketches for an edition of *The Princess*.

17 November T is in London, to protest at Moxon's publishing this book at Christmas, the designs being 'too wide of the text'.

20 November He returns from London with Mrs Gatty (who, after this first visit to Farringford, sends the Ts a copy of her short story 'The Poor Incumbent', followed by her *Legendary Tales* with her husband's sermons. She sends a scythe, which arrives on 1 Dec, when T uses it for the first time to cut his lawns).

December Jowett writes twice in response to ET's suggestion that he should recommend subjects suitable for poems, and tells her that he can send T any books from Oxford which she thinks may be useful. On the 24th Woolner arrives (staying into the New Year to complete a medallion of ET).

1859

6 January Jowett arrives (and stays until the 18th).

21 January The historian Henry Hallam, AH's father, dies suddenly.

15 February 'The Maid of Astolat' is 'quite finished now, all but last touches', ET informs Woolner. She has received her medallion, which T thinks could not be better. Mr Gatty, who had stayed with them from the 10th to the 12th, had 'proved to be an apparently open-hearted, kindly, sensible man'. (Late in the year he gives a lecture on 'The Poetical Character', illustrated from T's work, and published in 1860.)

21 February T and Emily finish reading the *Purgatorio* together.

March

23 (Wed) ET tells Woolner to assume that there will be no objection to Watts's including his portrait of T in the Royal Academy Exhibition unless he hears to the contrary before Sunday.

24 T is in London making arrangements for the publication of *Idylls of the King*. He does not object to the exhibition of his portrait.

25 He has been 'carried off' to Little Holland House, where he stays until early April to allow Watts time to complete his 'moonlight portrait' of him.

26 Woolner comes to hear him read 'The Maid of Astolat'.

April Possibly on the 10th, or later, C. L. Dodgson, who is visiting a friend at Freshwater, finds T mowing his lawn; indoors, ET is lying on a sofa, after a serious illness. He is invited to tea; afterwards he sees proof-sheets of the *Idylls* lying about, but T will not let him look at them (remembering perhaps D's parody of 'The Two Voices'; cf. Charles T's *Alfred Tennyson*, pp. 315–16). Next day D is at Farringford for dinner; he meets Sir John Simeon, and has a delightful evening. ET being too tired to look at his 'books of photographs', he leaves them, for collection the next morning. Late in the month, after spending Easter in the New Forest (he believed long afterwards it was in 1859), Montagu Butler, headmaster of Harrow, crosses over to the Isle of Wight, and calls on T.

9 May 'Riflemen Form!' is published in *The Times*, T warning Britain to be prepared for war, after the formation of the recent alliance between France and Russia.

23 May He hears that his bust, which has been at Cambridge with the publisher Macmillan, is now at Trinity College. The Duke and Duchess of Argyll dine at Farringford. (For a few days soon afterwards proofs are corrected in the summer-house.)

June

4 (Sat) Dodgson writes to ET about his photograph of Hallam, and asks (the question has been worrying him ever since he read the poem) whether 'Riflemen Form!' is T's work.

10 T travels to London with the proofs of *Idylls of the King*.

11 Edward Lear leaves Farringford after a few days' visit, during which he has sung to ET, and played after-dinner games with the boys. He is sorry for her, and wonders how much T, the sensitive poet, is alive to her suffering.

17 T reads 'Guinevere' to the Duke and Duchess of Argyll and Mr and Mrs Gladstone.

20 He attends a performance of *The Messiah* at the Handel Commemoration Festival in the Crystal Palace.

22 He goes to Little Holland House to have his portrait finished by Watts.

28 The day after his return home he reads the story of Sir Pelleas and Ettarre from Malory 'with a view to a new poem'.

29 Frederick T arrives from London, and spends much of his

time until he leaves on 4 July discussing Swedenborgianism with T. (Soon afterwards he leaves Italy with his family for Jersey.)

July *Idylls of the King* ('Enid', 'Vivien', 'Elaine', 'Guinevere') is published; Moxon & Co. have 40,000 copies printed. James Fields (of Ticknor and Fields, T's American publishers) arrives with his wife on the 14th, and stays two days, during which they hear *Maud* and 'Guinevere'. On the 16th 'The Grandmother' (for which T receives £100 without loss of copyright) appears in *Once a Week*.

August

6 (Sat) After staying several days at Park House, the Ts are with the Camerons at Ashburton Cottage.

16 T leaves his family behind, and travels with Palgrave and Brookfield to Southampton, where they are joined by P's friend F. C. Grove.

17 He sails with Palgrave and Grove for Portugal.

21 They reach Lisbon after a good voyage, and stay at the Braganza Hotel.

22 After driving round Lisbon in blazing heat, and viewing the Botanical Gardens, they can find no one to admit them to the Protestant Cemetery, where they wish to visit Henry Fielding's grave.

23 Cintra proves to be a disappointment: orange trees are dead of disease; streams have dried up; and the place is 'cockney', being 'crammed with Lisbon fashionables and Portuguese nobility'. T and Grove climb to the Pēna, a Moorish-looking castle on top of the hill.

28 In the evening (Sunday) they watch a bull-fight in Lisbon, not a blood-spectacle, but 'a trial of address'.

(The heat, the flies, the fleas, 'and one thing or another' make them decide to turn back, without having visited Seville, Malaga, Granada, and Gibraltar as planned.)

September

2 (Fri) They are waiting at Lisbon for a boat to Southampton on the 7th.

13 At Southampton they propose to spend the next two or three days at Lyndhurst.

20 At Cambridge T shows Palgrave AH's rooms (3G, New Court), the Backs, and the Jacobean brickwork of Queens' College. He spends the evening with his old tobacconist, and is engaged to dine with the publisher Alexander Macmillan the next day.

27 Emily, who has been very ill during the summer, travels from Park House (where her boys have been initiated in cricket) to meet Alfred in London.

28 At Farringford they meet Anne Weld (ET's sister) and her daughter Agnes (who are to stay with them three weeks).

October At Farringford from the 7th to the 10th Alexander Macmillan persuades T to let him publish, for £300, 'Sea Dreams' in his new magazine, which is to make its first appearance in November. On the 31st the Gattys arrive (staying until 5 Nov).

November

6 (Sun) T explains to Thackeray why he has delayed so long in replying to his offer. (Thackeray had wanted him to contribute to his first number of *The Cornhill Magazine,* which appears in January.) T tells him he cannot find anything worthy enough, after letting Macmillan have 'Sea Dreams'.

8 The Kingsleys arrive and stay two days.

14 Sir John Simeon dines with the Ts. (About this time the Ts hear that Woolner's plans for the positioning, pedestal, and lighting of the bust of T which is to be placed in the vestibule of Trinity College Library have been accepted.)

16 Sir John is coming today with Sir Charles Wynne. (Mrs Cameron is expected with her boys on Monday.)

During the month T reads Darwin's *Origin of Species* 'with intense interest'.)

2 December ET writes to placate the Cornish poet Stephen Hawker, after T had described the poem H sent in his praise, in addition to a volume of poetry, as 'too complimentary . . . to put faith in'.

12 December He agrees to a Tauchnitz edition of his poetry (published early in 1860).

By the middle of the month 'Tithonus' is finished, and there is snow two feet deep. Later the boys are delighted with Gilbert White's *Natural History of Selborne*, which Sir John Simeon brings them when he comes to dine.

1860

January 'Sea Dreams' appears in *Macmillan's Magazine*.

23 January The demand for T's poems has been increased by *Idylls of the King*. He is pleased to hear that the 75,000 copies of *The Cornhill Magazine* for February (containing 'Tithonus', a slightly revised form of 'Tithon', which T had written in 1833 as a pendant to 'Ulysses') were almost sold out 'some days ago'.

1 February Mrs Cameron, who has recently settled with her husband near Freshwater Gate, and named their home Dimbola, brings two legs of mutton to Farringford.

12 March ET thanks Mr Gatty for the gift of his lecture, sent by his wife, on the poetical character, illustrated from T's works. She has read it with much interest, but is 'too stupid and too coughy to write more about it'.

April

5 (Thurs) T informs the Duke of Argyll that Farringford has been invaded by whooping-cough, Emily having been kept to her room for six weeks; the worst is over, and he will defer his visit to town if the Duke and Duchess dare to come.

6 The Duke replies that they have no fears, having had whooping-cough, and will come to Freshwater next week.

11 Woolner promises to send 'the points of that Sailor's story' (from which T eventually writes 'Enoch Arden').

The Argylls stay at a hotel in Freshwater during the week, and visit the Ts three evenings. They tell T he must write 'The Grail' without delay. He recites his 'Boädicea' to the Duke as they walk in the cold through a stubble field in the neighbourhood.

17 T calls on his dentist in London.

19 At Macmillan's, in Henrietta Street, he inscribes his name in

capitals on the rim of the round table. (After midnight, when most of the guests have departed, he recites 'Boädicea'.)

May

17 (Thurs) Writing from Buckingham Palace, the Prince Consort requests the Poet Laureate to autograph the copy of *Idylls of the King* which he sends.

20 Henry Taylor comes to Farringford with Mrs Cameron.

28 ET is 'very glad' to see T's old Trinity friend Dr W. H. Thompson.

6 June The American missionary Dr Joseph Wolff, author of *Mission to Bokhara* (1845), arrives (and stays a week at Farringford).

16 June Edward Lear is on another visit, with Franklin Lushington, to the Ts. (For his benefit Mrs Cameron has her grand piano transported to Farringford by eight men.)

12 July Fitz insists that the Ts are to keep the Laurence portrait of T (which he had sent them years earlier) if they like it. (The recent exhibition of Watts's had made him wonder whether they wish to retain it.)

August

9–17 (Thurs–Fri) The Ts are in London, where they busy themselves with sight-seeing and visiting friends, before ET travels with the boys to Grasby (where they stay while T is on a tour to Cornwall and the Scilly Isles. His chief companion is to be Palgrave, whom ET has asked to take care of her short-sighted husband, especially when clambering over rocks. His continual concern irritates T, who persuades Woolner to stay with them as long as possible. The tour is of immense benefit to P, whose departure is delayed by his brother's arrival, for he discusses the preparation of an anthology of poetry with T, who is generous in suggestions and advice. The result is *The Golden Treasury* of 1861.)

18 At Oxford T meets Palgrave with his brother Gifford in Eastern dress, after recently escaping from his convent in the Syrian desert, where several of his fellow-monks were massacred. They dine with Woolner. (T shows that he is in a prickly mood during this visit. Jowett advises him not to

publish a new poem he has just read to him, and T retorts, 'If it comes to that, the sherry you gave us at luncheon was beastly.')

21 T and Woolner are at Bideford, after visiting Bath.

22 At Clovelly, 'the most picturesque gem' W has ever seen.

23 From Bude they travel to Boscastle and reach Tintagel.

25 Palgrave joins them there. Woolner, although he has much work in hand, is persuaded to accompany them further. (Subsequently they go to Camelford, and find Arthur's stone, T slipping into the stream in his eagerness to reach it.)

31 At the Union Hotel, Penzance, T is grieved to hear of the death of Lady Simeon.

September

1 (Sat) T writes to Sir John Simeon. They are at Land's End Inn (rackety and rather dirty) after 'four glorious days and *magnificently coloured seas*'.

6 He leaves Penzance for the Scillies with P, W returning to London.

20 After staying several days on the Lizard (at the Three Tuns), and leaving the two painters Holman Hunt and Val Prinsep (Thoby's son) sketching there on a promontory, they reach Falmouth (where they have a long talk with the diarist Caroline Fox on the 22nd).

23 They are at Perranporth, after staying at the Red Lion, Truro.

27 T returns home, five days after the return of Emily and the boys.

23 October T thanks F. J. Furnivall for sending him proofs of his (F's) edition of *Seynt Graal*.

November (early) Coventry Patmore, worn out with night-watching over his wife, stays for a short holiday with the Ts.

December (late) During Palgrave's visit T gives readings of the poems P has selected for *The Golden Treasury*.

(After her mother's death, Farringford becomes almost a second home to Louisa Simeon of Swainston. During her father's absences for his duties as M.P. in London, she could stay there as much as she pleased, and she went long walks with T. He taught her to know and appreciate Crabbe, whom he ranked high among English poets.)

1861

January Visitors at Farringford include the Bradleys of Marlborough College, the Bensons (E. W. Benson, head of Wellington College, made Archbishop of Canterbury in 1882), and Benjamin Jowett of Balliol College (already disturbed by the criticism he has encountered after contributing to *Essays and Reviews*, 1860), who talks of coming in the spring to work on Plato.

February

7 (Thurs) T leaves for another dental visit in London.

13 He returns after being much impressed by Lear's recent paintings.

17 He tells Emily about 'Northern Farmer' (the first of his poems in the Lincolnshire dialect), which he is planning.

18 By the evening part of it is written.

20 Henry Graham Dakyns arrives, to tutor Hallam and Lionel. He is twenty-three, 'said to be the most popular man in Cambridge', and highly recommended by those who knew him there and at Rugby; also by Granville Bradley and E. W. Benson.

28 T acknowledges the gift from William Barnes of his *Poems of Rural Life in the Dorset Dialect* (2nd edition, 1847), which arrived during his absence.

March Arthur Hugh Clough and his wife arrive at Freshwater to stay for six weeks. He is suffering from the disease which kills him later in the year, but is often at Farringford, playing with the children, and discussing with T the difficulties of translating Homer. On the 19th Lear dines with the Ts.

9 April Jowett leaves Farringford after a fortnight's visit. Franklin Lushington has been another guest. They have had so many uninvited callers they fear they will have to look for another house.

23 April Horatio and Charlotte arrive with two of their children,

Maud and Cecilia, after crossing the Solent in a thunderstorm.

May

16 (Thurs) On reaching Oatlands Park Hotel, Weybridge, on his way with his family to receive an honorary degree at Cambridge, T is afflicted again with heart palpitations, and decides to give up smoking (a resolution which does not last long). The journey is abandoned but, before leaving, T climbs St George's Hill with Hallam and Lionel for views of Windsor Castle and Hampton Court.

23 After walking several days in and around Winchester (Malory's Camelot), he expects to travel by train to London the next day. (ET and the boys have gone home.)

27 T returns briefly to Farringford. (He has invited the Welds to come, Charles having lost his post in April. They stay for about a month.)

1–5 June He visits the New Forest, staying at Lyndhurst, where he is joined by Edmund Lushington on the 4th.

27 June The Ts leave England for their holiday tour, after 'floods of visitors', Palgrave informs Clough. ET (who takes her maid) feels stronger, but the boys are still suffering the effects of whooping-cough.

21 July By chance they meet Clough at Mont Dore; he is on the way to Florence. T and Dakyns have climbed the Puy de Dôme and other extinct volcanoes. (From Mont Dore they travel to Tulle and Périgueux, 'a quaint place with its old Roman Tower and Cathedral with grass-green tower, church of St Etienne, and city walls', thence to Bordeaux. From Bagnères de Bigorre T climbs the Pic du Midi with Dakyns.

9 August The T party reaches Luchon in the evening; T is rather poorly again.

25 August Clough finds them in pleasant lodgings outside Luchon, near the river. T and Dakyns have walked a great deal, but the boys have not been well. They expect to be at Luz on Saturday (the 31st).

September

2 (Mon) They are there with Clough, who notes that T was at Luz with AH thirty-one years ago, and is very fond of the place.

6 'Today we *all* go to Cauterets', Clough writes.

7 The Ts are disposed to stay a week at Cauteretz. Clough walks with T to 'a sort of island' with pines on it, between two waterfalls, which T remembers from his visit with AH (it had furnished a simile in *The Princess*). Soon afterwards, in the evening, T writes his first version of 'In the Valley of Cauteretz'. (After a few days at Pau, where they had a sad parting with Clough, the Ts return home without delay – T feeling ill with a severe cold – via Tours, Paris, Amiens, and Boulogne. They arrive about mid-September. The news soon arrives of C's death in Florence.)

October (early) T completes his poem 'Helen's Tower' in response to a request from Lord Dufferin, who ten years earlier had built a memorial tower to his mother on a hill in his park near Belfast,overlooking St George's Channel, the Scottish coast, and the Isle of Man. (All it needs is *'a voice'*, Lord D wrote.) T also buys the Farringford farm (which is taken over on the 11th).

28 October He leaves for London (where he stays until 23 Nov, residing most of the time in Franklin Lushington's chambers, 2 Mitre Court Buildings. He pays several visits to his doctor, Mrs Cameron's brother-in-law, who prescribes chlorine baths and other treatment for the infection he caught at Cauteretz).

November

3 (Sun) He finds his mother (at Hampstead) very well. Frederick, who has brought his eldest son over to take an examination, is staying with her. (About this time T discusses the first draft of his ode for the International Exhibition with the composer Professor Sterndale Bennett; he hands the ode over on the 6th.)

9 He is one of the packed crowd in the Strand watching the Lord Mayor's Day procession.

11 In response to a a request made by T before leaving the Isle of Wight, Woolner brings his written account

of the fisherman story, which he had read on *The Queen of the South* when returning from Australia in 1854. He has recommended it to T on and off for about two years.

12 Browning (whom T saw yesterday, very pale with a silver beard) is coming to see him tonight.

December

5 (Thurs) At Farringford T has begun 'Enoch Arden', largely based on W's story.

10 He acknowledges the arrival during his absence of two copies of James Knowles's *The Story of King Arthur*. The book is dedicated to him, as the author wished when, on 13 August, he had sent part of the book in proof-sheets, which ET has read to Hallam and Lionel.

14 Albert, the Prince Consort, dies.

24 All the Ts go to Osborne (the Queen's residence on the Isle of Wight) as an expression of sympathy. T writes to Sir Charles Phipps, promising lines in the Prince's honour.

1862

January

2 (Thurs) Sir John Simeon brings his new wife to Farringford.

7 T forwards the 'Dedication' to his *Idylls* which he has written in memory of the Prince Consort.

9 He recites his Exhibition ode 'in a rolling voice'. (Lines 7–10 were added to the first draft as a tribute to the Prince Consort's work in promoting international exhibitions.)

13 T invites Sterndale Bennett to Farringford.

15 Princess Alice writes a letter of thanks for the 'Dedication', which has soothed the Queen.

25 He sends two copies of the 'Dedication' to the Duke of Argyll, one of them for Lord Dufferin.

6 February When Parliament assembles, Lord Dufferin in his eulogy of the Prince Consort quotes the concluding lines of T's 'Dedication'.

11 February T sends the Queen a copy of the new edition of the *Idylls* with the dedication 'To the Prince Consort'.

14 March At Farringford T reads 'Enoch Arden' to Lord Dufferin.

26 March In response to the Duke of Argyll's information that the Queen would like to see T the next time she is at Osborne, he writes, 'I am a shy beast and like to keep in my burrow'. He wants to know what kind of salutation to make when he enters her room, and how to make his exit.

April

14 (Mon) T travels with Jowett to Osborne, where he is received by Queen Victoria. She tells him that, after the Bible, her main comfort is *In Memoriam*, where the picture of AH reminds her of the Prince, 'even to his blue eyes'.

16 C. L. Dodgson lunches at Farringford, plays games with the boys, and tells them the Irish 'Mr O'Grady' story.

26 At Woolner's (29 Welbeck Street) T writes to Emily, telling her that Spedding is coming to hear him read 'The Fisherman' ('Enoch Arden').

29 He sees his mother, 'very well and hearty though almost bent double'.

30 He has refused tickets for the Exhibition, but goes to hear the choric rehearsal of his ode. Gladstone dines at Woolner's, and hears T read 'The Fisherman'.

May

1 (Thurs) The Great International Exhibition is opened, and T's ode is sung by a choir of 4000 to Bennett's music. Not wishing to join the procession, T is absent.

2 At the Duchess of Sutherland's invitation, he goes with Gladstone to spend the weekend at Cliveden (where he had met Lord Dufferin on the Sunday). From Simeon and others he has heard that the ode went very well.

7 He returns to Farringford with a young Wellingtonia tree, the gift of the Duchess.

14 June Henry Taylor hears 'The Fisherman' at Farringford, and finds it too painful, insufficiently 'glorified by imaginative power to exalt the reader above his terrestrial distress'.

July

1 (Tues) T helps with the haymaking. Mrs Cameron walks over the newly mown grass in the park 'looking gorgeous in her violet dress and red cloak'. It is pleasing to hear the men cheer, ET feels.

9 Coventry Patmore makes clear to the secretary of the Royal Literary Fund that his circumstances do not justify the request for a grant which the Ts have kindly made on his behalf.

10 ET tells Woolner that the story he has sent is 'very grand and very finely told'. (This is 'The Sermon', the source of T's 'Aylmer's Field'.)

18 The Ts travel to Ashburton Cottage (lent by the Camerons) for the start of their holiday.

5 August After staying with T's mother in Hampstead, they leave for Lincolnshire.

6 August T takes the boys to Lincoln Cathedral, on the way to Grasby.

August (second half) Leaving his family there, he travels with Palgrave in Derbyshire: Matlock, Haddon Hall, Chatsworth, Buxton (where they meet Monckton Milnes), Castleton and the Peak (so slighted by Scott in *Peveril of the Peak* that T cannot believe he was ever there), and Hathersage (with the reputed grave of Little John – Palgrave gives 'Robin Hood'). They move on to Yorkshire.

10 September T is back at Grasby, after visiting Ripon, Leyburn, Middleham Castle, Wensleydale, Bolton Abbey, and Skipton (where he leaves P on the 9th).

13 September After a very rough crossing, the Ts reach Farringford.

11 November In a letter to the Duchess of Argyll T protests against the unqualified laudation of Abraham Lincoln's preliminary Emancipation Proclamation by Charles Sumner (recently printed in *The Times*), and suggests that 'overproportion of Celtic blood' among the Northerners (in the States) accounts for their anti-British 'yelling and mouthing'.

29 November Watts finishes his portrait of ET (begun on the 21st), and begins one of T.

5 December T is working on 'Aylmer's Field'. 'He takes walks often now that the tourists are gone', ET writes to Woolner.

19 December 'We are all out transplanting Rhododendrons, we choosing places, the boys helping to dig', she notes in her journal.

1863

9 January Palgrave and his wife, after a brief honeymoon in Norfolk, arrive and spend a few days at Farringford; in the evenings she plays Mozart and Beethoven.

14 January The Queen's lady-in-waiting, Lady Augusta Bruce, brings T a copy of *The Prince Consort* from Queen Victoria. Hallam gathers snowdrops for her, almost all of which she presents to the Queen.

March

6 (Fri) In response to a request that he should provide lines in honour of the arrival of Princess Alexandra of Denmark, who is to marry Edward, Prince of Wales, T sends the Queen at Osborne a copy of 'A Welcome to Alexandra'.

10 The poem appears in *The Times*, to coincide with the wedding at St George's Chapel, Windsor. T receives his admission ticket too late to attend. Farringford celebrates with flowers, Danish and English flags,a cake, a torchlight procession, a bonfire on the down, and a dance after supper.

11 Mrs Gatty comes with her son Stephen.

16 At Osborne T and Emily express their good wishes for the Prince and Princess of Wales.

April

1 (Wed) Charles Weld, a superintendent of the Exhibition, brings an inscribed urn and salver in acknowledgment of T's 'Ode Sung at the Opening of the International Exhibition'.

10 T reads 'Aylmer's Field' to Emily and Jowett.

23 A Roman urn with coins is found in the Terrace grounds

(of the house which the Ts had bought and furnished to save their view of the sea), during operations for the creation of a mound.

9 May The Ts visit Osborne by invitation, and Hallam and Lionel are presented to the Queen.

11 May A messenger brings a gift of books from the Queen, including Guizot's translation of Prince Albert's speeches, with her album, in which she wishes him to write something. He inscribes 'In the Valley of Cauteretz', which he knew she had enjoyed hearing the Duke of Argyll read.

June

11 (Thurs) From Farringford T writes to Robert Bridges (a future Poet Laureate), a sixth-form student at Eton who, for his recitation of a passage in *The Princess*, has been rewarded with a portrait and an autograph of T, and has written him a letter of thanks, thinking him the donor. Daniel Conway, an American in England to give a favourable impression of the Northern States, and a Browning admirer, makes a memorable call.

24 Watts's portrait of ET arrives while the Duke and Duchess of Argyll are present.

27 T travels with Mrs Cameron to London, where he is to stay at Little Holland House.

28 Thackeray and his daughter Anne come to see him. He is suffering from an inflamed leg, the result, he believes of the vaccination he had undergone to please the insistent Mrs Cameron.

July

1 (Wed) Browning (widower since 1861), William Rossetti, and William Bowman see him in the evening.

2 He visits the exhibition of pictures by the old masters at the British Institution.

3 Watts is working on another picture of him (for Bowman).

10 After consulting other doctors, he sees James Paget. He suffers from gout and eczema, and is being moved to the Palgraves' (York Gate, Regent's Park).

24 He is still at P's, where he has been in a highly feverish

state. His doctors have ordered him to go to Harrogate for spa treatment. (In London his visitors have included, in addition to Browning, Sir John Simeon, Spedding, Carlyle, J. A. Froude, and Holman Hunt.)

August At the end of the month, after travelling with his family to York, Ripon, and Fountains Abbey, he is at Harrogate, where he has been confined to his bedroom for two weeks. More than three weeks pass before he recovers. On the 31st ET orders more bottles of 'the Amontillado' for him.

September

10 (Thurs) T journeys to London.

11 Here he meets Emily and the boys (who have travelled from Grasby). Their driver overturns his cab while making a sudden turn, and they are lucky to escape with only scratches and bruises.

12 They see T's mother at Hampstead.

14 While crossing over to the Isle of Wight, they are joined briefly by William Allingham, who is on his way from Lymington (where he is the customs officer) to lunch with Mrs Cameron and meet Henry Taylor.

October

3 (Sat) WA leaves Lymington on the 3 p.m. boat, and visits the Ts with Mrs Clough, and with Frederick Pollock and his son.

4 He returns the next morning by invitation, and after lunch is taken to T's 'den' on the top floor, then up a ladder to the leads, where T is accustomed to watch the heavens. (One night, while gazing at shooting-stars, he had tumbled through the hatchway, and fallen ten feet, the ladder fortunately saving him from serious injury.) T tells him that the original of the dark yew 'sighing for Lebanon' in *Maud* was at Swainston (Sir John Simeon's).

24 T is still working on 'Aylmer's Field'. ET longs for him to begin 'The Holy Grail', 'feeling sure that is his work and the days are going fast for him and me'.

1 November Fitz hears news of the Ts from W. B. Donne, who has enjoyed his visit to the Ts (on 10 Oct).

26 November Mr Wilson, Dakyns' successor, arrives. D had gone to teach at Clifton College in September.

December

20 (Sun) WA lunches at Farringford; all take part in wheeling ET to the top of High Down.
23 Lady Augusta Bruce and Arthur Stanley are married in Westminster Abbey. The T boys hoist flags and fire caps in their honour.
24 W. M. Thackeray dies.
26 WA accepts an invitation to Farringford, and finds Palgrave there; after dinner they discuss classical metres.
27 They walk with Hallam and Lionel along High Down to the Needles.
28 T, P, and WA walk to Alum Bay and look at the coloured cliffs. The Bradleys of Marlborough and the Butlers of Harrow join them for dinner, after which the subject of classical metres is continued at length; ET grows tired of it.
30 Granville Bradley and his wife go to Farringford in the 'white evening'. T recites in a rolling, swift, and musical manner 'The Voyage', and says the poem is a great favourite of his.

(Late one afternoon, before the year's end, in bitter weather, with snow lying on the ground, Annie Thackeray and her sister arrive, to stay in one of the Dimbola cottages lent them by Mrs Cameron. They are resting in twilight by the fire when T arrives 'in silent sympathy'.)

1864

February

9 (Tues) From London, to which he travelled the previous day, T writes to Emily; he has arrived safely at Spedding's, and received the manuscripts of his poems, including 'Enoch Arden'.
11 He dines at Pollock's (59 Montagu Square) with JS, Tyndall, and the astronomer (Sir John) William Herschel.
12 He dines at Palgrave's, and hears his brother talk about his Eastern travels. Gladstone is one of several who call. T recites 'Northern Farmer, Old Style'; he and P witness

Browning's signature to copies of his will, and there is talk on the education of boys, G being very decided on the urgency of sending Hallam T to school.

16 T's letter to Emily makes clear one of the main purposes of his London visit: to hear his friends' views of the poems he thinks of publishing.

17 After dinner at Woolner's T reads 'The Aylmers' and 'The Lincolnshire Farmer' ('Aylmer's Field' and 'Northern Farmer, Old Style'), JS, P, and Pollock being additional guests.

18 He dines at Gladstone's, where he meets J. A. Froude, editor of *Fraser's Magazine*.

24 He is busy with proof-sheets.

26 He has 'all the things' printed, but means to 'keep them at present'.

28 The Duke of Argyll calls, and T reads 'The Voyage'.

1 March T returns to Farringford.

24–8 March WA is at Farringford for Easter. Jowett, who is staying with two students at a neighbouring house, calls on the Ts every day. Walter White (secretary and librarian of the Royal Society from 1861 to 1884) arrives on the 25th, and finds Laurence making a crayon portrait of T.

5 April They all go to see Garibaldi, a popular hero after the liberation of Italy, who is staying at Brook with the Seeleys. (A few days later he comes to Farringford, where a large crowd has gathered. He plants the Wellingtonia tree which the Duchess of Sutherland had given T, and mistakes Mrs Cameron for a beggar-woman as she kneels and implores him, her hands blackened with photographic chemicals, to be photographed at Dimbola. Garibaldi sends T a copy of Foscolo's *Poesie* from London, and T sends him *Idylls of the King*.)

24 April Fitz thanks ET for the engraving of T from Watts's portrait which Laurence has sent him; it is not very like the T he remembers.

Early May (?) About this time T hears that his aunt Mary Bourne has died, and thinks she would have tried to see him had she not become most wayward and violent. He answers his nephew

Giulio (Frederick's son) on the subject of Garibaldi's visit, and congratulates him on gaining his lieutenancy in the British army.

24 May The T boys put up flags, and the family has plum-pudding, in celebration of the Queen's birthday and the anniversary of Charles and Louisa's wedding-day (cf. 1836).

28 May Martin Tupper calls and gives ET a copy of his works.

June

6 (Mon) T takes Hallam and Lionel across to Lymington; they visit Beaulieu Abbey with Allingham.

15 T is in London (at Woolner's) to discuss the publication of *Enoch Arden, and Other Poems*, and for further treatment of his gout. (A correspondence on the title ensues between Emily and T, who, after holding out for 'Idylls of the Hearth', 'Idylls, Chiefly of Seventy Years Ago', or 'Home Idylls', accepts her first choice.)

19 Pollock breakfasts with Woolner to meet T and JS.

26 A copy of Charles Turner's *Sonnets* (1864) reaches Farringford.

27 The Welds and Henry Sellwood have bought Aubrey House, Keyhaven (on the mainland opposite the west end of the Isle of Wight), in order to be near the Ts. ET takes her boys to see it, and they are all delighted with it.

29 Lionel, who has 'taken possession' of his uncle's *Sonnets*, enjoys reading them to his mother about this time.

6 July T returns home, after staying in London to hear Gladstone in the debate on the Schleswig-Holstein question. (The Speaker allowed him to attend on Monday the 4th.)

August

3 (Wed) To escape the tourists again, the Ts leave Farringford for London on the first stage of their holiday.

6 They leave for Boulogne, on their way to Brittany and Normandy.

11 They have come to Chartres from Paris. (After proceeding via Le Mans, Angers, Nantes, Carnac, and Quimper, they visit Lannion to see Keldthuen – where Arthur is said to have held his court – and Avalon. In the country from Quimper to

Morlaix they find a 'wild Wales in miniature' on their way to Mont St-Michel.)

September

2 (Fri) They see the Bayeux Tapestry.

3 At Caen they stay a long time listening to music in the Abbaye aux Hommes.

6 They are at Rouen. (In the meantime *Enoch Arden, and Other Poems*, published in August, has sold amazingly well. It is T's most popular volume. The 'Other Poems' include 'Aylmer's Field', 'Sea Dreams', 'The Grandmother', 'The Northern Farmer, Old Style', 'Tithonus', and 'In the Valley of Cauteretz'.)

9 From Dieppe they return to the Isle of Wight.

10 Gerard Manley Hopkins, in a letter to A. W. M. Baillie, illustrates the 'Parnassian' style in poetry from Tennyson, whom he has begun to doubt; he quotes from 'Enoch Arden'. (The Parnassian is the manner in which great poets have come to see and describe things 'without further effort of inspiration'.)

October

1 (Sat) ET's father leaves Farringford with Louisa and Charles Turner.

8 WA crosses the Solent for Farringford, where he meets the publisher Macmillan and Mr and Mrs Pollock

14–17 Edward Lear becomes tired of Mrs Cameron's intrusions, and of T's 'ravings about England "going downhill" '.

22 The Pollocks spend the evening at Farringford, where they hear T read 'Boädicea' and 'The Lincolnshire Farmer'. In answer to P's question, he says he prefers 'Enoch Arden' to 'Aylmer's Field', which he put aside six months because the story was 'so intractable'.

26 It had been hoped that Hallam and Lionel would have gone to Charles Kegan Paul (the future publisher), near Wimborne, for tutoring, but as ET would not allow their long curls to be shorn, lest they catch cold during the winter, he has refused to have them until Easter.

November

5 (Sat) Emily convinces T that they must find a second home for peace in the summer, and favours Surrey, where she had lived with her father.

12 Mr Wilson, Hallam and Lionel's tutor, leaves (his successor, Mr Lipscombe, having arrived the previous day).
19 T returns to Woolner's, partly to check the publication of a selection of his poems in sixpenny parts, dedicated to the working men of England.
20 He tells Walter White that Moxon's manager expects to sell 50,000 copies. The sale of more than 40,000 copies of his 'Enoch Arden' volume has already brought him over £5000. The encroachment of building-schemes on Farringford is making him consider a move.
26 He visits his mother at Hampstead, and finds her looking exceedingly well. Arthur T and his wife are there.
28 He has heard of ninety acres for sale (offered to Walter White) at Haslemere for £1500.

31 December 60,000 copies, the whole of the first impression, of *Enoch Arden, and Other Poems* have been sold.

1865

14 January *The Athenaeum* reports that T has accepted a baronetcy from the Queen.

31 January As no baronetcy has been offered him, T has no difficulty in answering a letter on the 'pros and cons as to acceptance or refusal' from Frederick Locker, Lady Augusta Stanley's brother-in-law.

February Despite the adverse weather, efforts are being made to raise a bank on which to grow a screen of trees blocking out the new red-brick houses which ruin the view from Farringford.
18 (Sat) 'I hear you have got something new to match the *Lincolnshire Farmer*', the Duke of Argyll writes. This is 'Northern Farmer, New Style'.
20 Woolner is at Farringford, hoping a rest will cure the inflammation which affects one of his eyes.
21 T hears that his mother is ill.
22 Hearing that she is much worse, he sets off for Rose Mount, the home at Hampstead he has rented for her since she left

Twickenham. She dies before his arrival, and he hasn't the heart to see her.

25 He decides he will stay at his brother Arthur's until the funeral.

27 Mrs T is buried in Highgate cemetery; T wishes it could have been in a country churchyard.

14 March Proposed by the Duke of Argyll, he is unanimously elected to membership of 'The Club' (Dr Johnson's Club).

20 March ET tells Woolner, who has written suggesting a house near Seaton, that she prefers the Surrey hills for a summer home (remembering her 'paradise', as T calls it, at Hale near Farnham, before her marriage). About this time T congratulates Swinburne on his recently published *Atalanta in Calydon,* although he admits his objections to parts of it; it is long since he read anything so fine.

6 April WA and T call on the Camerons. At Yarmouth the former meets the two Miss Thackerays, who have just landed and are on their way to Freshwater (where they meet Jowett and his four students, all at Dimbola cottages).

May

2 (Tues) Mr Lipscombe, the T boys' third tutor, leaves to teach at Winchester.

6 T writes 'To Dante' for the sixth-centenary birthday celebrations (in response to a request from Florence).

15 He writes to Aubrey de Vere on the death of his old friend Stephen Spring Rice.

22 After being kept at home by whooping-cough, Hallam and Lionel, shorn of their locks, are taken to be educated by Kegan Paul, vicar of Sturminster Marshall. On the way, the Ts stop to see the minster at Wimborne.

23 Arthur Munby sees T and (he supposes) ET on the 4.30 p.m. steamer to Lymington.

June

5 (Mon) T writes from Hampstead.

8 T and Emily return via Winchester, where they stay the night.

24 WA visits Farringford after his visit to Ireland. The publisher Mr King and his wife are the Ts' evening guests. After dinner

they talk about public schools, and the effect of a few bad boys on the rest.

25 After dinner, and claret in the drawing-room, WA goes to the top of Farringford alone. When he returns to the drawing-room, he finds T about to read to the Kings, and with them he listens to the whole of *Maud*.

July (early) T is at Woolner's for a short London visit. On the 9th he recites 'Northern Farmer, New Style' after breakfast with Woolner, Walter White, JS, and Pollock. They are later joined by Macmillan, Laurence, the painter Arthur Hughes, and G. M. Fenn, who talks of getting Gustave Doré to illustrate an edition of T's poems.

23 July Professor Richard Owen, the naturalist, arrives at Farringford, and T accompanies him to Brighstone, where they examine a Saurian reptile dug up at Brook. Owen has never seen one so sheathed in armour, and thinks it might be called Euacanthus Vectianus (signifying its unearthing on the Isle of Wight).

9 August T takes his family for a holiday in Belgium and Germany.

13 August They continue the examination of the field of Waterloo which they began on the 12th. (They stay in Brussels a week, then move on to Luxembourg and Trèves [Trier], which they find enchanting, with its cathedral and Roman remains, including the palace of Constantine the Great. They row down the Moselle (with, no doubt, recollections of Charles's sonnets here, as at Trèves) to Koblenz, which T dislikes as much as ever. At Weimar they see the palace rooms where Goethe lived; also Schiller's house.)

September

1 (Fri) They visit Goethe's house in Weimar. (They then proceed to Leipzig, and the following day to Dresden, where three visits are paid to the picture-gallery, Raphael's *Madonna and Child* being the main focus of attraction.)

6 After viewing the armoury at Dresden, T takes his boys to the gallery again.

7 They travel by train to Brunswick, where T and the boys

visit a church crypt to look at the coffins of nine Dukes of Brunswick who all fell in battle.

10 They reach Aix-la-Chapelle (Aachen) in the evening, the city looking magical with domes and hills gold and blue in the sunset.

12 They return home.

28 Queen Emma of the Sandwich Islands is received at Farringford. T walks with her on the down.

30 WA is presented to her at Farringford.

October

1 (Sun) As she wishes to see the Needles, T drives with her for the view.

2 He gives her two large magnolia blossoms on her departure.

6 He reads Emily 'some Lucretius' (part of the poem which he completes in 1868).

19 At Farringford T tells WA that Weimar, where he touched Goethe's coffin, is 'the most interesting place in Europe'.

November

1 (Wed) WA takes the Dorset poet William Barnes to Farringford. B and T are soon happy together, talking about the ancient Britons, and prehistoric barrows and roads.

8 T has heard that his aunt Elizabeth Russell has remembered him in her will.

19 After crossing on the 18th, WA and Woolner breakfast at Farringford. They stroll to the top of the down before lunch. (Matilda T is now living with her maid at Farringford; she is to spend much of her time there, some at Grasby.)

24 Mrs Gatty arrives with her daughters (and stays until the 29th).

December

1 (Fri) T leaves for London, where he stays at Woolner's.

3 They call on Froude; all three walk on to see the Carlyles. Mrs C is glad to see T, who thinks she looks very weak. (She dies at the end of the following March.) C thinks T has 'a dilapidated kind of look', though he is 'cheerful of tone'.

4 T calls twice on Queen Emma, who is leaving the next morning for the Continent.

6 After dinner at Woolner's, he moves to the Palgraves', where he dined the previous day. Perhaps it is after his removal, late in the evening, that Milnes (now Lord Houghton) calls with Swinburne, after making arrangements for him to meet T. Swinburne talks briefly with him, then moves into the next room and becomes engaged in a long talk with Palgrave and G. H. Lewes on the art of William Blake and Flaxman, much to the annoyance of the Poet Laureate.

7 T is 'inducted into' the Royal Society after 'a merry dinner with lots of anecdotes'.

8 T dines at Woolner's with Gladstone, Holman Hunt, and Dr Symonds, a Bristol physician. He asks Gladstone to speak to Lord Russell on an increase in WA's pension. When (after dinner) the doctor's son, John Addington Symonds, arrives, they are discussing Governor Eyre's brutal quelling of a mutiny in Jamaica; unlike Gladstone, T sympathizes with the Governor. On the subject of panic, he says he could be brave if suddenly faced with danger but not if he had time to reflect. Palgrave arrives, and turns the subject to newspapers, T all the while sipping port. After reference to the coming Reform Bill, coffee is served, and T is left to smoke. On leaving the dining-room, Woolner gives G the manuscript book containing T's Homeric translations; T is invited to read them but refuses, and is displeased that G has been scrutinizing them. After discussing the universe, and repeating the Pauline view that there can be no urge towards moral good ('the crown of man') without a belief in immortality, T agrees to read his translations. (He later accepts G's objections to the use of 'Jove' and 'Greek'; cf. 'Achilles Over the Trench'.)

13 He calls on Tyndall, and has a long chat with him on mind and matter. He then dines with H. H. Milman, Dean of St Paul's.

14 Like Browning, he is one of 'a great gathering' at Woolner's which includes John R. Thompson, the American writer and Confederate (editor of *The Southern Literary Messenger*), with whom T had corresponded in 1851.

(T becomes friendly with Norman Lockyer, who has a six-inch equatorial telescope in his Hampstead garden. During his future London visits they meet several times to discuss the latest astronomical discoveries and theory.)

19 ET writes to Woolner to say that 'Alfred has arrived safely this morning by the 12.30 boat', after sleeping at Lymington and dining and breakfasting with WA.

31 He writes '1865–66'.

1866

January

3 (Wed) Jowett and Matilda T ('Tilly') depart. 'Seldom can two so good go from any house', ET writes.

5 Mr Dakyns comes for a week. Everyone is delighted to see him.

8 T rebukes J. B. Payne, the manager of Moxon's, for his discourteous language about Ticknor and Fields, his American publishers. They have sent him £250 for the year, and he has no wish to break with them. Mr and Mrs Fields are his friends, and have visited him at Farringford.

20 Hallam T leaves for his first term at Marlborough, the school chosen by T because his friend Bradley is the head, and Arthur Stanley, Dean of Westminster, told him it was the best in England.

February

1 (Thurs) From his custom-house WA sees T on the incoming steamer. He meets him, and walks with him while ET and Lionel pay a short visit to Aubrey House. The Ts are on their way to London for their first long holiday together there, staying at Upper Gore Lodge, the home of ET's aunt Lady Franklin.

4 With the Carlyles they lunch at the Deanery, Westminster. Dean Stanley takes them to see Thackeray's bust in the Abbey.

10 The Brookfields and their daughter Magdalen join them for the evening.

15 Spedding, Venables, and Brookfield dine with the Ts. The party which follows is attended by the Argylls, Lady Boyne, Mrs Gladstone, and others. JS, V, and B stay on to smoke with T.

17 At a reception given by Lady Stanley of Alderney, T meets Browning, Lord Houghton (Monckton Milnes), and Carlyle.

March

5 (Mon) John R. Thompson calls at Lady Franklin's in the evening, and finds T ill with a severe cold but cordial. He meets several eminent people there, including Woolner and Macmillan.

14 T, still suffering from influenza and lumbago, has to give up his engagements. (Other friends met by the Ts during their London stay include the Maurices, the Gardens, Edmund and Franklin Lushington, Forster, Palgrave, Froude, Mrs Clough, the Prinseps, the Simeons, the Marshalls, Gladstone, Lord John Russell, and d'Eyncourt cousins.)

22 ET and Lionel (on the day before they return home with T) drive with Mrs Carlyle and her 'fatal little dog' (an allusion to the circumstances of Mrs C's death a month later, 21 Apr).

May

1 (Tues) T takes Hallam to Marlborough, where he is the Bradleys' guest.

2 They visit Avebury and Silbury.

3 T begins 'The Victim' (which he finishes the next day). In the evening he reads 'Guinevere' to the Upper Sixth.

5 He returns to Farringford.

10 He takes Emily to seek medical advice in London.

12 They return to the Isle of Wight.

18 ET is still unwell. WA is at Farringford, and T tells him how, when he heard of the death of Byron, he went to the back of the rectory at Somersby, and cut on a wall with his knife 'Lord Byron is dead'. He thinks Byron was popular because he wrote vulgarly; he himself is popular because he is the Poet Laureate, 'something like being a lord'.

29 T writes from Farringford to Emily, who is in London to consult her doctor.

13 June WA breakfasts at Farringford. (Other visitors about this time include Woolner and Henry Taylor.)

30 June John R. Thompson and J. B. Payne visit T at Farringford.

July

15 (Sun) The Ts, including Hallam, are at the Crown Hotel, Lyndhurst, where they are joined by WA. He and T walk in the woods. They sit on the roots of a huge beech, and T

smokes; after sandwiches and brandy, he reads aloud from *As You Like It*. (WA has further walks in the New Forest with T until the 22nd.)

18 T and Hallam walk to Romsey Church.

25 The Ts go to Aubrey House.

August

1 (Wed) T and the boys take Emily to see the reapers cutting barley and oats in their breezy fields at Middleton (on the west side of Farringford).

6 To celebrate T's birthday (which he generally does not like his family to observe), a dinner is given to his farm men.

17 WA and his friend Edward Burne-Jones ('Ned') cross over to Farringford; T takes them up to his 'den', and talks on the qualities which displease him in Swinburne's poetry.

20 Following Charles Kingsley's recommendation, the Ts take Lionel to Dr James Hunt of Hastings for his general education and a course of speech therapy (to cure his stammering).

4 September They are at Park House, where (anxious to avoid sight-seers at home) they have spent about two weeks.

16 September From Petersfield, still looking for a site on which to build a summer residence, they look at land to be sold, then at the Devil's Punch Bowl, Hindhead. They had planned a holiday in Switzerland, but have been deterred by bad weather, and by the fear that Lionel might catch cholera and be sent home.

October

11 (Thurs) T agrees to consider a proposal made by George Grove that he should write a song cycle similar to Heine's.

16 James T. Knowles, author of *The Story of King Arthur and His Knights of the Round Table*, calls at Farringford. T being out, he is invited to return in the evening. He is taken to the attic, where T talks on King Arthur, 'as being a subject of common interest and sympathy'.

17 George Grove and Arthur Sullivan spend the afternoon and evening at Farringford. Some of the songs are finished, and they try them out on 'a *very tinkling* piano, very much out of

tune', before retiring to the top room, where T reads the songs and other poems, then talks on the next world and God and man until 2 a.m.

November

3 (Sat) The Ts go to Haslemere, but Mrs Gilchrist (widow of Blake's biographer) insists they stay with her while they try to find land for building a summer home.
8 They are at Stoatley Farm near Haslemere, still prospecting.
15 They return after visiting Grayshott Farm.
22 T reads 'Window Songs' or 'The Loves of the Wrens' (already privately printed) to WA, saying 'They're quite silly' and jumping around, at one point, 'like a cock-pigeon'.

December An agreement is reached to rent rooms at Grayshott Farm near Haslemere for two years.

1867

January

15 (Tues) 'Ici on parle Français' is acted by Mme de Lacy, the Camerons, and the T boys. The Camerons act admirably, ET thinks. Her boys have been skating, sledding, shooting, and walking.
25 WA crosses the Solent, and takes the field-path to Farringford, where he finds ET (looking ill) and Matilda T in the drawing-room. He walks on the downs with T, who is unhappy on the question of man and his destiny; T, he discovers, loves the spirit of Christianity but hates many of the dogmas.
28 T sends a copy of 'Elaine' with illustrations by Gustave Doré to the Queen (as a result of which he and Emily are invited to Osborne between 7 and 20 Feb).

February

1 (Fri) WA finds the Ts much the same.
2 He takes a long walk with Lionel to the end of the downs overlooking the Needles.
3 T tells him that he was deterred from the pursuit of his

Arthurian epic by John Sterling's review of 'Morte d'Arthur' (Sep 1842).

8 Arthur Sullivan comes, and discusses the songs with T. (He stays until the 11th, plays Bach on Emily's piano, and sings two of his own songs.)

15 T visits the Queen at Osborne, and they talk about Doré (whose illustrations of the *Idylls* he is receiving); Emily is unable to attend.

1 March A telegram informs the Ts of Hallam's illness. They catch the next boat, reaching Marlborough the next day. (Later they telegraph for Dr Symonds of Bristol. The way to the sanatorium has to be cleared by a snowplough.)

14 March The Ts are still at Marlborough; ET writes a letter to Lionel for his birthday. (Hallam is brought home on the 26th.)

3 April WA, who is staying at an inn, helps T to transplant primroses. T makes punch unsuccessfully, after dinner, from whisky and claret.

29 April The Ts move to Grayshott Farm for the early summer, hoping to find a site for a new summer home.

May

18 (Sat) T takes his boys to Gilbert White's Selborne, where they climb the Hanger.

24 Drummond Rawnsley comes.

26 WA finds the farmhouse where the Ts are staying at Grayshott, and meets Palgrave there. He is taken by Lionel to the secluded site his father thinks of buying.

June

5 (Wed) The Ts visit the site on Blackdown for their new home, Lionel on a donkey, his mother in a basket-carriage (which has to be lifted over ruts). It is a 'charming ledge on the heathery down' with an extensive view over the Sussex Weald. (Later Edward Lear comes to Grayshott from Liphook, and would like the Ts to 'look out for some land for him hereabouts'.)

16 The Blackdown land is bought. By chance T meets James

Knowles at Haslemere station. He suggests that K, an architect, design his house. K agrees on condition that he does the work without a fee, his reward being the pleasure he has gained from T's works.

29 The Ts return to Farringford.

17 July T, his brother Charles and Louisa Turner, Matilda T, Hallam, Lionel, and two daughters of Frederick from Jersey travel by boat with WA to see the British and French fleets (a demonstration of an *entente cordiale*) at Spithead. The Queen visits the French fleet. The day is overcast and showery; there is a firework display before their return to Yarmouth, WA continuing his return to Lymington on the same boat.

August

5 (Mon) He meets Bradley and others at Farringford.

23 He crosses by steamer to Yarmouth, where he meets T (and Frederick T and his two daughters, on their way to Grasby). T invites him to go with him to Lyme Regis, knowing that Palgrave is there with his family, and having wished to see the Cobb ever since he read Jane Austen's *Persuasion*. WA agrees, and they travel by train (second class) via Ringwood, Wimborne, Poole, and Wareham to Dorchester. They walk through stubble fields, seeing reapers at work, to Maiden Castle. Having booked for the night at the Antelope, they go up the back yard to the Museum, where they examine British antiquities and Roman pottery. They then walk through the meadows by the river, with a view of the county gaol, which looks like 'a pleasant residence'. After having dinner with a pint of good port, they visit the poet Barnes at Came vicarage (where WA had stayed a year or two before) in the twilight; he is delighted to see them.

24 From Bridport they walk via Chideock and Charmouth to Lyme Regis.

25 T walks along the Cobb before breakfast. Afterwards he returns with WA, who reads to him the passage describing Louisa Musgrove's fall. Palgrave continues the tour with T, and they walk to Beer Head, where they have a fine view of the Devon coast to Start Point.

12 September After exploring parts of Dartmoor and the Salcombe peninsula with P, T returns home, and finds Hallam there, after an outbreak of scarlatina at Marlborough.

19 September He leaves with Emily to see Henry Sellwood (who dies in his sleep the next morning) at Aubrey House, Keyhaven.

8 October WA visits Mrs Cameron's, where he meets Henry Taylor and his daughter Emily. After lunch he calls on T, who tells him that England is 'going down' and Christianity dying out.

4 November Fitz, writing to ET, expresses surprise that T approves of his 'old Omar'; he had not expected him to know about it, and declares he would never have sent him a copy, always assuming that 'he would not approve anything but a literal Prose Translation'.

25 November WA is met at Yarmouth by the T carriage. He has lunch at Farringford. Mrs Clough comes with her daughter and maid.

December

1 (Sun) T brings down 'The Higher Pantheism' for Emily to read. (A day or two later he drops a copy of 'Wages' – perfected during the night – on Louisa Simeon's breakfast-plate. During the month copies of 'The Song of the Wrens' ['The Window'] and 'The Victim', privately printed by Sir Ivor Guest, the Canford Press, Dorset, are received, and folio editions of 'Vivien' and 'Guinevere', illustrated by Doré, are published for Christmas. T has been learning Hebrew, and reading it in Job, the Song of Solomon, and Genesis.)

24 WA (who is staying at Myrtle Cottage until the end of the year) is the Ts' sole guest at dinner; T 'rages against the Fenians'.

27 He tells WA that the *Odyssey* is 'the most delightful book in the world', and blank verse 'the only English metre to translate Homer in'.

28 WA, Woolner, and W. G. Clark of Cambridge dine with the Ts. (Other visitors during the Christmas–New Year season include the Simeons, Jowett, and then the Bradleys.)

1868

January

1 (Wed) 'The Victim' appears in *Good Words*, T receiving £700 for it. (Anxious perhaps over the cost of his new summer residence, he changes his policy over periodical publication significantly this year, finding it most lucrative.)

3 George Grove, now editor of *Macmillan's Magazine*, on his visit to Farringford, offers £50 for 'Wages' and £300 for 'Lucretius' (terms confirmed by Macmillan on the 6th).

10 The T boys and Henry, Mrs Cameron's son, act in *Box and Cox*.

11 T talks of publishing 'The Lover's Tale', lest someone who has one of the written copies in circulation should forestall him. 'Allowance must be made for redundance of youth', he says. (During the year he completes an additional part, 'The Golden Supper', for the poem, a trial edition of which is published in 1869.)

20 T receives from the Queen an inscribed copy of her *Leaves from the Journal of our Life in the Highlands*.

24 He discusses the origin of 'The Lover's Tale' (from Boccaccio) with the Bradleys.

25 He tells Granville Bradley how much he wishes he had regular work like him, finding time hang heavily when he is not engaged in a long poem. He is now reading the Song of Solomon in Hebrew.

29 At Farringford, after an evening performance of *Box and Cox* in the drawing-room, there is dancing, T leading off with Lady Simeon.

31 T leaves for Haslemere; he and Knowles are to fix the site for the new house, to be called Aldworth after the name of a Berkshire village where ET's Sellwood ancestors belonged. (Afterwards he goes to K's home, The Hollies, Clapham Common.)

February

'Wages' appears in *Macmillan's Magazine*.

2 (Sun) T attends Westminster Abbey to hear Dean Stanley preach.

9 He and Woolner are at Cambridge as guests of W. H. Thompson (now Master of Trinity) and his wife. He meets the public orator W. G. Clark and the geologist Professor Sedgwick, and calls on the Persian scholar Edward Cowell, who, after a period in India, had been made Professor of Sanskrit, largely through the influence of Thompson when he was Vice-Chancellor.
22 Venables visits Farringford (and stays until the 25th).

8 March Jowett writes, advising T not to publish in magazines.

28 March The Ts meet Thackeray's younger daughter Minnie and her husband Leslie Stephen. Writing in June, Stephen said that they had stayed a month at Freshwater, and made the acquaintance of 'the queer old poet' T. (About this time an unusual amount of pollen-smoke is observed in the yew trees, and section xxxix of *In Memoriam* and the speech of Ambrosius in 'The Holy Grail' – cf. 11. 18–19 – are written.)

April
10 (Fri) T walks with WA to the Beacon (at the top of High Down, overlooking the sea), and entertains him with Lincolnshire stories.
13 After hearing from Moxon's manager that his general sales have declined in recent years as a result of the book-post importation of cheap Tauchnitz editions, T writes to the Prime Minister (Disraeli) and the Privy Council asking whether preventive measures can be taken.
17 The Monteiths come with their two daughters.
23 It is Shakespeare's birthday, and T chooses it for laying the foundation stone of Aldworth. Few, apart from the Simeons and Mr and Mrs Knowles, are present at the ceremony.
26 Frederick Pollock visits Knowles at Clapham to meet T, who is staying there. There is much talk about publishers with whom T may publish.
30 At Knowles's, Tyndall and Pollock hear T read from *Maud* after dinner.

May 'Lucretius', bowdlerized a little, appears in *Macmillan's Magazine*. Drummond Rawnsley and his wife stay at Farringford from the 19th to the 28th, and tell some very amusing Lincolnshire stories. On the 24th they all go to Charles Pritchard's to observe Venus and the moon through his telescope.

6–10 June Gifford Palgrave is a guest. One evening he performs the Muslim service and call to prayer.

19 June T and Emily leave for Ryde and Haslemere. (After seeing work in progress at Greenhill [Blackdown] for Aldworth, they stay at Clapham Common; they see Macmillan and Mr Craik, and their – the Ts' – solicitor Arnold White.)

July

16 (Thurs) The American poet Henry Longfellow and his party (ten in all) lunch at Farringford.

17 Forty or more are invited to meet him at tea, and he talks to all of them in turn.

20 The Ts are on their way to London, where T has an appointment with his dentist. WA travels with them to Brockenhurst. They call at Eton College to enrol Lionel, he not being strong enough to endure the winters at Marlborough.

24 From Ross-on-Wye they visit Goodrich Castle.

25 After driving to Tintern Abbey, they proceed to Chepstow and Caerphilly Castle.

August

10 (Mon) WA finds T sitting at a small table on the lawn 'with books and tobacco'.

12 T helps Hallam with his Latin.

17 Charles Darwin calls and assures T that there is no conflict between his theory of evolution and Christianity.

31 At Brockenhurst WA meets Aubrey de Vere on his way to Freshwater.

September

3 (Thurs) At Farringford, de Vere talks on Catholicism, 'sliding into Newmanism and Jesuistry', the Ts being 'mildly dissentient'.

9 T reads aloud to Emily 'a bit of his "San Graal" ["The Holy Grail"]', which he has recently begun.

14 It is almost completed, and ET is 'pleased to think that the

Queen and the Crown Princess wished him to write it'. 'It came like a breath of inspiration', she writes.

23 The Ts take Lionel to Eton. In the garden, at Mr Warre's request, the poet reads the whole of the manuscript 'San Graal'.

25 Returning, they cross the Solent in a heavy gale.

October

13 (Tues) T writes to Gladstone on the alleged mistreatment of Fenians in prison, enclosing *Lays of a Convict*.

17 WA calls, and he and T visit Mrs Cameron.

19 They walk with Mrs Ritchie, her three daughters, and Annie Prinsep, to Afton Down and Brook Point, the barrows on the former and the fossil trees at the latter being of special interest.

21 They visit the Needles, Mrs Ritchie and Annie Thackeray driving with ET.

November

7 (Sat) Horatio T brings his two daughters to Farringford for a few days after the death of their mother.

13 In London T calls on Lear, and makes arrangements to sever his links with Moxon's. His new publisher Alexander Strahan dines with him at the Knowleses', where he is staying. A discussion in the evening between Charles Pritchard, Knowles, and T originates 'The Metaphysical Society'.

19 He calls on Lady Franklin and Sophy Cracroft. At the novelist Emily Eden's, he and Knowles participate in an attempt to move a table mesmerically. Browning calls and returns with them for dinner, after which T reads 'The Holy Grail', which RB declares T's 'best and highest' work.

23 T has sent the whole of 'The Lover's Tale' to the press, and is to have it back on Thursday. The agreement with Strahan is ready for signature.

December

2 (Wed) T and Frederick Locker start their visit (postponed from the previous Saturday, mainly because the 'Golden Supper' proofs arrived days late) to Paris (where they

have a leisurely holiday, visiting the Louvre, the museums, churches, and markets; they return to London on the 12th).

24 T writes from Headon Hall, Alum Bay, where Emily is staying with Hallam and Lionel while Farringford is scoured and disinfected, after one of the maids had contracted typhoid fever.

31 In a letter to Strahan & Co., he stresses that the £4300 annual payment guaranteed by the agreement dated this day is to be reduced to £4000 if Mrs Moxon dies while the contract holds, 'except in respect of additional works as provided in the agreement'.

1869

January T reads 'The Holy Grail' to the Bradleys, 'explaining the realism and the symbolism, and how the natural, if people cared, could always be made to account for the supernatural'. On the 15th Charles Weld dies suddenly, and T's 'connection of 37 years' with the Moxon publishers terminates (though for many years T allows Edward Moxon's widow an annuity – initially £300 – without disclosing its source). He receives a cheque for £500 from J. T. Fields, his American publisher. Having failed to find either the Duchess or the Duke of Argyll at home, T writes to the former on the 27th, indicating his wish that the Duke should become president of their new club, which is to be called 'The Metaphysic and Theological Club' or by some such name. Questions which 'agitate and perplex' the age are 'to be freely discussed and handled by men of all religions and metaphysical shades of opinion'.

6 February 'The Turners are with [the Welds] and are as good angels to them', ET writes to Edward Lear.

February (late) 'The Coming of Arthur' is completed. T is reading Robert Browning's *The Ring and the Book*.

2 March Anne Weld arrives with her daughter Agnes. (They are to stay on the island; their furniture is housed temporarily in the Terrace stables.)

3 March Charles Merivale sends T a translation of Homer which he has had the audacity 'to do into English rhyme' (probably an early portion of his *Iliad* translation, published in 1878).

April

20 (Tues) From Haslemere the Ts visit their new house with James Knowles.

21 T attends the inaugural dinner of the Metaphysical Society at Willis's. ET takes Lionel to Eton. (The Ts are staying with the Knowleses, and driving into town every day to buy furniture for Aldworth.)

26–9 They are at Marlborough, with Hallam and the Bradleys.

12–18 May Mr and Mrs Knowles stay at Farringford; he has the power to encourage T in his work, ET believes. 'Pelleas and Ettarre' is well under way.

26 May Invited to Farringford, WA has great pleasure in accompanying Miss Mabel Lowell 'in her first walk in English fields'; an old cottage almost covered with ivy surpasses everything. Miss Lowell, daughter of James Russell Lowell, is from Massachusetts; she has come with Mr Fields and his wife. (They stay from the 25th to the 27th.)

June

2 (Wed) The first meeting of the Metaphysical Society takes place under the presidency of Sir John Lubbock at the Deanery, Westminster. T does not attend, but his poem 'The Higher Pantheism' is read. (Pollock used to say that the Society was formed to convince T of the immortality of the soul.)

14 T leaves Folkestone with Frederick Locker and the Revd Stenton Eardley of Emmanuel Church, Streatham, for Munich and Switzerland.

19 Having travelled via Basle and Zurich to Interlaken, they leave for Lauterbrunnen, and walk up to Mürren. Looking at the higher Alps, T suggests that all visible phenomena are the shadow of the Almighty, a distorted shadow to which we are restricted by the limitations of our senses.

26 From Wengern Alp Hotel they walk down to Grindelwald (where they stay until Tuesday, enjoying close views of the glacier, avalanches, and streams).

July

1 (Thurs) They reach Lucerne by carriage from Brienz.

2 Mount Pilatus being clouded, they hire a boat and rowers for an excursion on the lake, but have great difficulty in returning, the rowers being tired, and the visitors taking an oar in turn.

7 They reach Paris, after staying at Strasbourg and Rheims, where T has been much impressed by the cathedral.

10 They breakfast with the painter Gustave Doré at the Moulin Rouge.

12 Pollock, keen to meet T again, joins the Lockers at 91 Victoria Street, London, for dinner.

6 August At Aldworth nothing pleases T more than the bath; he has three baths a day, he tells Locker, acknowledging his present of a Guercino and a 'magnificent Marc Antonio print'.

1 September ET likes the solitude at Aldworth, but prefers the beauty of Farringford. Her sister Anne is at Farringford with her daughter; they are having a home built in the neighbourhood. The Turners are probably there too. (All four come to Aldworth on the 20th; Lear leaves on the 28th, tired of T's self-centredness.)

October

Early this month WA visits T at Aldworth, and enjoys the 'magnificent prospect' from Blackdown.

7 (Thurs) The terrace is almost completely levelled, and the laying of turf (all from Farringford Down) has begun.

17 Locker, who has just returned from Aldworth, writes to T on a pirated edition of 'The Loves of the Wrens', pieced together by R. H. Shepherd from Barron Brightwell's recent T *Concordance* and a borrowed copy of the private edition.

19 Dr and Mrs Acworth come, and practise spiritualism. T and his sister Matilda are amazed by table-rapping, and a table 'heaves like the sea' in his study.

November

5 (Fri) Still at Aldworth, T is revising proofs for *The Holy Grail and Other Poems*. Palgrave arrives.

9 T goes to town on publishing matters (returning on the 15th).

16 He will attend 'the Metaphysical dinner' tomorrow, ET thinks.

26 He goes with Locker to check proofs in London.
29 ET and Matilda have been alone at Aldworth since Friday. Matilda recalls how the news of AH's death reached Somersby, and, one evening just before his death, the appearance of a tall figure in white which vanished through a hedge at a point where there was no gap.

December

The Holy Grail and Other Poems (dated 1870) is published by Strahan & Co. Beside the title-poem, the volume includes 'Lucretius', 'The Coming of Arthur', 'Pelleas and Ettarre', 'The Passing of Arthur', 'Northern Farmer, New Style', 'The Golden Supper', 'The Victim', 'Wages', 'The Higher Pantheism', and 'Flower in the crannied wall'. *Idylls of the King* (the eight Arthurian idylls) is also published.
4 (Sat) Pollock visits T at Aldworth, two days after the latter's return.
10 After days of cold raw mist at Aldworth, the Ts are happy to reach Farringford.
17 Lionel, recovered from measles, returns from Eton.
21 Hallam arrives from Marlborough.

1870

January

1 (Sat) A letter from James Knowles on the *Idylls* appears in *The Spectator*. (Although T was to feel that it 'explained some things too allegorically', he described it as the best and only true critique of the *Idylls* that had appeared.)
11 T has 'written sharply' to Strahan because it does not appear he has paid the £4300 due on the 1st, and T does not know how to pay the bills for furnishing Aldworth.
19 He informs Spedding that he has taken chambers in London (Albert Mansions) for three years; they are yet to be furnished.
25 The Ritchies and Anne Thackeray dine with the Ts.

March

1 (Tues) Hallam, who contracted chicken-pox a few days after Christmas, and has not yet returned to Marlborough,

has been reading Virgil with his father; they are now studying the fourth book of the *Aeneid*.

15 T leaves for Aldworth and London, where he remains two weeks, visiting friends and acquaintances. His latest volume of poems has proved to be a great success.

27 Lord Houghton informs his aunts that he has the great honour of entertaining the Poet Laureate, who insists on having port, at dinner tomorrow.

28 George MacDonald (who, on 25 Aug 1865, had asked T to support him for the Chair of English Literature and Belles Lettres at Edinburgh University) invites T and Emily to watch the Oxford and Cambridge boat race from his house (The Retreat, Hammersmith) on 6 April, and bring their friends.

April WA gives up his customs post at Lymington, and moves to London as sub-editor of *Fraser's Magazine*.

May

9 (Mon) T and Hallam drive to Swainston, but arrive too late to see the Simeons, who have left for Switzerland.

23 The Ts are just starting for Aldworth when they learn that Sir John Simeon has died at Fribourg.

31 T leaves Aldworth to attend his old friend's funeral. While waiting for the procession to form at Swainston Hall, he begins composing 'In the Garden at Swainston'. He returns in the evening.

June

13 (Mon) After dinner on his wedding-anniversary, he goes with Mr and Mrs Knowles by train to London, where he stays in his new rooms.

14 He attends the funeral service for Dickens in Westminster Abbey; at the end people flock towards the altar in order to get a good view of him.

15 In the evening he takes the chair at the Metaphysical Society meeting.

27 He replies to Lady Simeon, accepting any memorial of her husband, 'the very Prince of Courtesy', she chooses to send or bring. He invites her to Aldworth on 4 July, and Louie, any time.

July

1 (Fri) 'We are still knee-deep in guests to be and Papa is going again to town. . . . Aunty Nanny and Agnes go tomorrow. Mr Jowett has been here since Wednesday . . . Lady Simeon is to come on Tuesday. . . . Papa does not settle here one bit', Emily informs Hallam from Aldworth.

15 T has seen Paget about his eczema and gout.

26 ET and Hallam travel to London to bring him back to Aldworth. Lady Augusta Stanley, with her sister Lady Charlotte Locker (Frederick's wife), takes them in her carriage to the station for the return journey. T has heard that war is declared between France and Germany.

August

7 (Sun) Charles Turner and Louisa arrive. (Before they leave Aldworth on the 17th Emily Jesse comes. With Matilda they have a 'large family party'.)

8 ET informs WA that T has been unable to walk for two months, and has 'spent a great part of the time a prisoner to bed and pain'. He tells a correspondent that he thought he had invented the stanza for *In Memoriam*, but had since found it in Ben Jonson and, only the other day, in two stanzas by Lord Herbert of Cherbury.

10 Mrs Sabine Greville, a wealthy and eccentric elocutionist, theatre enthusiast, and admirer of T's poetry, reads 'The Grandmother' most dramatically.

29 Edmund and Cecilia Lushington come with their daughter (and stay until 14 Sep).

18 September T tells Leslie Stephen, who has walked over from Bramley near Guildford, that 'none of the damned cockneys can get near him' at Aldworth.

27 September Louis d'Eyncourt (T's cousin) comes with his wife. Mr Garden arrives.

21 October ET writes to Hallam at Marlborough, saying that Papa is tired of guests owing to his long confinement.

November

4 (Fri) Arthur Sullivan comes with Knowles and Mr Strahan to

discuss the publication of T's 'Window Songs'. (T reluctantly decides to publish and honour his agreement with AS, and they appear with AS's music in December.)
12 Lady Franklin comes with Sophy Cracroft from Moor Park, Hertfordshire, for luncheon.
18 T has had to decline the Royal Society's invitation to join their trip to Cádiz, where they expect to view the eclipse. They had hoped he would write a poem on the subject.

10 December Sir Frederick Pollock meets T at the Knowleses', Clapham; after dinner T reads the sermon from 'Aylmer's Field'.

16 December He returns to Emily at Farringford.

1871

February
16 (Thurs) T receives from Jowett, now Master of Balliol College, his translations of Plato's dialogues in four volumes.
22 'Poor Ally has had a dreary eight or nine months rather from eczema in the leg and the treatment for it', Emily writes to Lear. He has never recovered from the loss of Sir John Simeon, she tells him.
24 Mrs Cameron has sent T Swinburne's new volume (*Songs Before Sunrise*). He describes it as 'blasphemous'.
26 He speaks 'despondingly of Swinburne's book and of the tone of literature in his set', and forebodes the 'fiercest battle' between 'good and evil, faith and unfaith' (ET's journal).

24 March The Ts visit Anne Weld in her new house; she has a beautiful view.

During the spring T has a library built on the south side of Farringford, with a playroom or ballroom below.

May
1 (Mon) Anne Thackeray, who has been a visitor during April, leaves. T is writing 'Sir Tristram' ('The Last Tournament').
4 Jenny Lind (Mme Goldschmidt) dines at Farringford.
12 She sings some of the *Elijah* magnificently, and ET concludes

that she is deeply religious. At T's request she sings 'Auld Lang Syne' and 'Auld Robin Gray'.

24 He reads 'Tristram' to Emily. He had often discussed plans for the poem with her, and she thinks it 'very grand and terrible'.

June

5 (Mon) Fitz writes, telling ET that if she feels as he does she must tell Laurence (who had taken it for cleaning the previous year) to send back the picture of T 'swept and garnished with a suitable Frame', and hang it where she can see it. It is the only one of the earlier Alfred, and, without a beard, 'which makes rather a Dickens' of him in the photographs, the best of all his portraits.

7 The Scottish poet Robert Buchanan writes from Oban, hoping that T can give him much needed financial assistance.

14 He writes gratefully to thank T for his 'noble aid', promising to repay as soon as possible.

16 Hallam arrives at tea-time, after taking entrance examinations at Trinity, Cambridge. (He had been persuaded to do this by his new headmaster F. W. Farrar, his parents having given up the idea of Trinity because they thought 'the lowlier and safer lot of a small college' more suitable for him.)

20 Buchanan writes to acknowledge receipt of T's cheque for £200.

22 T takes Hallam to the Royal Academy; they return in the evening.

27 The Russian novelist Turgenev stays with the Ts at Aldworth; he plays chess with W. G. Clark and Hallam before leaving the next day.

July

9 (Sun) T, at Little Holland House with Mark Pattison, Watts, and others, meets Pollock in the afternoon. (About this time he makes the acquaintance of Edmund Gosse at the British Museum, where G is employed. T refers graciously to Gosse's recently published poems, and they talk about Norway, which G is about to visit.)

14 G. H. Lewes meets T on the train from London, and takes him to see George Eliot at Shottermill near Aldworth. T thinks she resembles Savonarola.

16 The Pollocks arrive to stay two nights at Aldworth.
18 Mrs Clough comes.
22 T and Hallam drive to meet Mr and Mrs Gladstone. A telegram arriving to say they would come on a later train, they fill in the interval by calling on the Leweses (G. H. Lewes and 'George Eliot'). In the evening T reads 'The Holy Grail' at the Gladstones' request.
29 Mrs Sabine Greville, Fanny Kemble, and Lord Houghton come for lunch. Fanny Kemble reads Shakespeare, with tears streaming down her cheeks. As they drive away up the hill, she is heard telling Lord H to get down off the box: 'you are no inconsiderable weight'. T rejoices that the National Education Bill is passed; there should be no franchise without education, he believes.

August

7 (Mon) He and Hallam set off for North Wales. (They climb Snowdon, and return on the 16th.)
9 Lewes and George Eliot call at Aldworth, and find Emily with Lionel.
26 T walks with George Eliot to Shottermill. Emily follows and stays for a time, after which he reads *Maud* and 'Northern Farmer'.
31 He visits the Leweses (the day before their departure), and reads 'Guinevere', which makes GE weep.

September

16 (Sat) After staying with the Howards at Naworth Castle, east of Carlisle, T is with his cousins at Brancepeth Castle, which he finds 'rather triste' by comparison. Robert Bonner writes, offering T £1000 for a poem, 'even if not more than twelve lines in length', for the January number of *The Ledger*, New York.
19 T returns unexpectedly to Aldworth.
30 Farrar assures ET that Hallam will suffer no disadvantage in going to Trinity at Christmas.

October

4 (Wed) Charles Turner and Louisa arrive.
9 W. H. Thompson, Master of Trinity, writes to say that he will 'relax the rule'. He hopes to see Hallam after Christmas;

it would be painful if one with such a name did not come to Trinity.

14 On their way to Lyme Regis, the Palgraves stay at Aldworth.

15 Charles enjoys Palgrave's talk on Shelley, Keats, Wordsworth, and other poets. T reads Wordsworth in the evening, 'and we had a general service of reverence to that great poet', wrote P (who had included many poems by W in *The Golden Treasury*).

16 The visitors depart, Charles looking 'so fragile that it makes one count the days with him', ET writes.

November
During the first week the Ts spend a few days at Oxford, dining at Balliol, and meeting the Bradleys, who invite Hallam from Marlborough. (Granville Bradley is now Master of University College, Oxford.)

11 (Sat) James Knowles and the scientist Thomas Henry Huxley arrive at Aldworth. T agrees with the latter on the subject of George Eliot's humility, despite an assertive manner in her more recent writings.

16 Robert Buchanan sends T a copy of his new play *The Drama of Kings*, which he regards as an experiment in literature.

25 Farrar writes, telling ET that Hallam has won the reading prize (his second during the half-year); he rejoices that he is ending his course at Marlborough so happily and so creditably.

28 Buchanan writes, requesting another £100 from T: his play will not bring him a penny.

December T and Emily leave Aldworth for Farringford on the 5th; Mrs Cameron greets them at Lymington station. 'The Last Tournament' appears in the December number of Knowles's *The Contemporary Review*, a Strahan publication.

1872

January

6 (Sat) T's poem 'England and America in 1782' (twenty lines adapted from an early poem, and forwarded on 10 Nov in response to Bonner's offer of £1000) appears in *The Ledger*, New York.

19 Charles and Louisa arrive; her sister Anne has been very ill.
21 R. W. Emerson writes from Concord, hoping that T will allow his daughter to meet him when she is in England with her husband, Colonel Forbes.

19 February T and Hallam drive to Osborne to leave 'our names on the Queen's book and the Prince's' (ET writes) as an expression of gratitude for the Prince of Wales's recovery from typhoid fever.

22 March Charles and Louisa leave Farringford. Mrs Cameron comes to bid them farewell.

March (late) To Fitz's question whether he preferred the first or second edition of his *Omar*, T answers that he cannot find his copy; he admired it immensely, and supposed it was the first, adding that Fitz stole 'a bit in it' from 'The Gardener's Daughter' (a statement which causes a rapid increase in correspondence between Fitz and T until the latter admits his mistake).

April
By this time T is friendly with W. G. Ward, who, a year or more earlier, had come to live in his new house, Weston Manor, on a hill half a mile or more to the west of Farringford. Their friendship was slow to begin, though Ward was, like T, one of the founder members of the Metaphysical Society. He had become an extreme Roman Catholic, a firm believer in papal infallibility. The Ts disagreed fundamentally with his religious bigotry, but he admired ET's spiritual strength, and T shared his faith in divine guidance and immortality. He was stimulated by Ward's lively intelligence, enjoyed his humour, and appreciated his kindliness and sincerity.
3 (Wed) Hallam leaves Marlborough.
8 F. W. Farrar, who had hoped that his parents would visit the school before H's departure, writes to tell ET that he is proud of having had him at Marlborough.
17 T regrets that he is unable to comply with a personal plea for financial assistance; he has parted with more than £1800 to one of his family in the last few months.
28 He writes to his friend Frederick Locker, on hearing of the death of his wife Lady Charlotte, after apparent recovery

from a painful illness. He and Emily will be pleased to see him at Farringford whenever he can come.

20 June The Ts travel to Aldworth (where T works on 'Gareth and Lynette').

23 June He replies to 'Lewis Carroll', thanking him for his recommendation; he does not, however, think it worth while to send Lionel to Sheffield for a speech-cure 'lecture' from Dr Lewin.

9 July T goes to London (where he remains some time, partly to make final arrangements for the publication of 'Gareth and Lynette' with 'The Last Tournament').

15 July T returns to Aldworth with Mrs Brookfield.

August

1 (Thurs) Spedding is a guest at Aldworth.

7 The T family leaves for a holiday in France. (In Paris they hear about conditions during its recent siege by the Prussians. T takes Hallam and Lionel to the Louvre, where he admires Velázquez's portraits immensely. He buys several volumes of Victor Hugo and Alfred de Musset.)

14 Leaving Hallam at Fontainebleau to study French with Pasteur Brand, the Ts proceed to Dijon (then to Mâcon and Vienne, where Emily is delighted with the Gallo-Roman remains. It is a wonderful day for T when they drive along the Isère valley to Grenoble, with a magic, dreamy light on the distant crags of the French Alps).

21 From Grenoble T visits the Grande Chartreuse with Lionel.

29 From Aix-les-Bains they climb the Dent du Chat (6000 feet high), and gain a superb view of Mont Blanc, which T thinks looks like 'a great cathedral with three naves'. The guide says they are both good mountaineers.

September

2 (Mon) They are at Geneva.

5 They begin their return journey (via Lausanne, Paris, and Amiens) to Aldworth.

24 T sends Strahan his corrections for *Gareth and Lynette, etc.*

October

7 (Mon) Mary Ker (T's sister) arrives with her husband and son.
8 Hallam leaves Aldworth for Trinity College, Cambridge.
24 A review of the recently published *Gareth and Lynette, etc.* – comprising only T's last two Idylls – appears in *The Times.*
27 Knowles calls. To his question 'what he thought he had done most perfect' T answers 'Nothing', only fragments such as the two songs 'Come down, O Maid' and 'Tears, idle tears'.
29 T attends, with Hallam, the wedding of Louisa Simeon and Richard Ward, then goes to stay with Knowles at Clapham.
31 Knowles is going to see Strahan about the publication of more sonnets by Charles (Tennyson) Turner.

November

2 (Sat) Pollock dines with T at the Knowleses'.
3 Knowles and T call on Allingham. K invites him to dinner, during which T recites Lincolnshire nursery rhymes.
7 The publisher Henry King dines with T at K's.
12 T attends the meeting of the Metaphysical Society.
13 Writing to Dr W. C. Bennett, T thanks him for his flattering poem, and wishes he had what Swinburne calls 'the divine arrogance of genius', so that he could accept it and 'rejoice abundantly'; he is reminded, however, of Marvell's 'Time's winged chariot' and 'Deserts of vast eternity'.

December

5 (Thurs) He returns to Farringford via Ryde.
6 Work is begun on arranging T's books in his new study.
25 ET makes a copy of the dedicatory epilogue 'To the Queen' for *Idylls of the King.*
28 G. F. Watts writes from Little Holland House; he is glad to know that his new home (The Briary) will not disfigure the neighbourhood of Farringford.

1873

13 January Granville Bradley calls to say goodbye. The play at the Camerons' has been a success, Lionel's acting and Hallam's singing being much praised.

15 January T and Emily call on Richard and Louisa (*née* Simeon).

February

3 (Mon) 'Poor Papa has not a soul to speak to now for Mr Ward is gone away for some weeks', ET writes to Hallam.

15 T goes to stay with the Lockers in London (where he is to meet Hallam).

20 He writes to say that he attended the Cosmopolitan Club the previous evening. He dines with Knowles.

26 The Queen writes to thank T for his copy of 'the very fine new edition of "The Idylls of the King" ' and for the 'beautiful Epilogue'. She invites him to Windsor, where she will show him the mausoleum containing Prince Albert's remains whenever he is near. (The reference is to the 1873 Imperial Library Edition of T's works, published by Strahan in 1872–3; for this T divides 'Enid' into two idylls.)

March

4 (Tues) Anne Thackeray and her sister Mrs Stephen call on T in the morning.

6 T visits Windsor Castle, and walks with the Dean (of Westminster) and Lady Augusta Stanley to Frogmore, where they wait for the Queen to show them Prince Albert's tomb.

9 He meets Mr Markham, secretary of the Hakluyt Society, who gives him information about Sir Richard Grenville. T wishes to write a ballad on his fight in *The Revenge* against the Spanish. (His poem 'The Revenge' was written in 1877, after he had rediscovered Edward Arber's 'English Reprint' on the subject.)

10 T returns from London, after an absence of more than three weeks.

16 He informs Dean Stanley that he does not prize any honour from the Queen except so far as it is a symbol of her kindliness. He would prize it for his boys' sake (i.e. if it were hereditary).

17 Three distinguished scientists visit T at Farringford: Professor John Tyndall calls with Huxley, who shows wide interests and talks on *In Memoriam*; he comes again with Sir Joseph Hooker (President of the Royal Society), and they stay for tea.

19 T walks 'most days' (ET writes) with Agnes Weld, who is 'merry as a bird' and very informative.

21 He is pleased with Lord Dufferin's letter from Ottawa on the happy effect of 'true North' in the Epilogue to his *Idylls*.
25 T receives Gladstone's letter, offering him a baronetcy from the Queen.
30 He replies, saying he would rather it were reserved for his son Hallam.

c. 13 April Mrs Richard Ward invites T and Hallam as Easter guests at their Freshwater home. They meet Mr and Mrs Leslie Stephen (Mrs Stephen, Anne Thackeray's sister, died on 28 Nov 1875).

16 April T accepts Henry King's publishing proposals in a general way, leaving the details to be settled between him and Arnold White. (King is the former partner of Strahan, whose business has failed. His contract will guarantee T £5000 p.a. for five years on books in print, with a 5 per cent commission on new publications.)

May
8 (Thurs) T receives from Browning a copy of his recently published *Red Cotton Nightcap Country*.
9 He reads Milton to Mrs Cameron, Annie Prinsep, and Anne Thackeray.
11 Anne Thackeray dines at Farringford, and T reads passages from the Bible at her request.
28 Arthur T arrives with his wife Harriet.

11 June Lionel leaves to take his entrance examinations at Cambridge.

July
18 (Fri) The Ts move to Aldworth.
20 T goes with his sons to a garden-party at Lady Franklin's.
31 Aubrey de Vere comes; his conversation is affectionate and delightful.

2 August T reads 'Vivien' during the Pollocks' two-night stay.

11 August He sets off with Hallam (on the latter's twenty-first birthday) for Alpine Italy.

September

4 (Thurs) Hallam notes that T has begun 'The Voice and the Peak', after a beautiful early morning view of Monte Rosa.

5 From Ponte Grande they go to Domo d'Ossola. Later they cross the Simplon Pass. His expectations heightened by Wordsworth's lines, which relate to the Gondo gorge – not the Simplon Pass – in wild weather, T is disappointed.)

10 On their homeward journey, they reach Neufchâtel, where talk among foreigners is mainly on the Tichborne trial.

29 The Bradleys come with their two daughters to spend a few days with the Ts at Aldworth. (Other visitors about this time or later include Arthur Hallam's sister Julia, and the poet and critic Roden Noel.)

October

7 (Tues) T begins reading aloud in the evening from Shakespeare. By the end of the week he has read most of three of his plays.

13 Hallam leaves for Trinity College, taking Lionel with him for his first term.

18 Mrs Greville arrives while the Ts are on the terrace watching the preparation of Emily's rose-garden.

27 Mrs Craik (Miss Mulock, author of *John Halifax, Gentleman*) comes with her husband to see Matilda T ('Tilly').

28 T and Emily go to London, where they stay with Lady Franklin at 4 Seamore Place.

November

8 (Sat) Venables is one of their guests at dinner.

10 (probably) Hallam and Lionel having arrived in the meantime, T takes them and Annie Ritchie to see Irving in *Richelieu*. (T goes daily to Woolner's, in preparation for his draped bust of 1874.) They see Dean Stanley and his wife Lady Augusta.

11 Carlyle dines at Forster's with Spedding and T, whom he finds 'distinctly rather wearisome; nothing coming from him that did not smack of utter indolence' or torpor, though enlivened by tones of 'boylike naïveté and total want of malice', except against unfavourable reviewers.

15 Accompanied by Mrs Cameron, her son Henry, and Mr Knowles, T goes to Cambridge to see his sons and friends.

('He had lunches and dinners, and walks with Trinity fellows and undergraduates, and was as happy as a boy', Hallam remembered.)

17 He returns to London with Knowles.

December

F. J. Furnivall invites T to be President of the Shakespeare Society he is forming, but he declines the honour. He takes Hallam and Lionel to see Carlyle. With Hallam he sees Helen Faucit (Lady Martin) in *As You Like It*. The Ts entertain and meet many friends, including the Brookfields, Ritchies, Leckys, Sir Frederick and Lady Pollock, Allingham, Anne Thackeray, Mrs Greville, Mrs Clough, Mrs Anne Procter, and Andrew Clark.

16 (Tues) T attends the Metaphysical Society dinner.

19 Browning dines with the Ts. 'He was very affectionate and delightful', Emily wrote.

23 The Ts return to Farringford.

29–31 The Thompsons (from Cambridge) lunch with them.

1874

January

Early this month T is continuing to read Shakespeare to his company in the evenings.

15 (Thurs) T's contract with his new publisher Mr King takes effect.

25 He begins the reading of *Othello* (and later abandons it because it is too tragic).

February

4 (Wed) T has been walking with Agnes Weld in the mornings, and reading *Henry IV* to Emily in the evenings.

5 The Prinseps come to live at the Briary, G. F. Watts's house near the Farringford estate.

19 Drummond Rawnsley and his wife Kate leave after a short stay at Farringford.

March

1 (Sun) Andrew Clark thanks T for the present he has sent; no gift he has ever received will be more precious, and no event

in his professional life has given him more pleasure than the opportunity of ministering to T's personal comfort.

6 T writes to Lord Houghton, his 'old college comrade, of more than forty years' standing', to sympathize with him on the loss of his wife. 'The nobler nature does not pass from its individuality when it passes out of this one life', and she will live in her children, he is moved to write.

12 On this wintry day T and Knowles have seats in Regent Street to greet the Duke of Edinburgh's bride, daughter of the Tsar of Russia. For this occasion he had written the lines 'A Welcome to Her Royal Highness Maria Alexandrovna, Duchess of Edinburgh', which had been published in *The Times* on the 7th.

21 He dines at Lady Franklin's and meets Henry Morton Stanley, 'the Livingstone finder'.

April For some time T, realizing the public response to historical drama, after the success in London, the previous year, of W. G. Wills's *Charles the First*, has been considering historical subjects. By the end of the month, after studying Holinshed, J. A. Froude, and ecclesiastical histories, he has sketched two or three scenes for his play *Queen Mary*.

12 July His old friend W. H. Brookfield dies; cf. T's tribute 'Brooks, for they call'd you so'. (About this time probably he and Hallam visit Stratford-on-Avon.)

August He visits France with his family; the weather is generally too cold for Emily, who stays at Tours with Lionel. In Paris they attend the Théâtre Français. From Tours T travels with Hallam to the Pyrenees, where they climb almost to the top of the Pic du Midi d'Ossau.

September (early) They walk in and around the valley of Cauteretz, and visit Pont d'Espagne, where T and AH met Spanish revolutionary leaders in 1830. ('Not much of a tour', T reiterated in his letter to Palgrave on 16 Oct.)

On returning soon afterwards, Emily became very ill, largely through having to answer numerous letters, particularly from unknown correspondents who asked for advice on religious questions or criticism of poems. The result was that she was unable to continue her journal, which T had wished her to keep for his convenience. A later consequence was the withdrawal of Hallam from Cambridge to help his father 'in reading books for him, writing letters, and in his work generally'.

8 October Edmund Lushington, after a family loss and funeral, finds 'The Voice and the Peak' 'quite new, and . . . like a wild and mighty psalm, in truest harmony with all our present thoughts and feelings'.

16 October T informs Palgrave that Emily is 'still obliged to lie flat', and that her doctor has said she 'must not exert herself in any one thing' if she is to recover. (She was to spend much of her remaining life in this state.)

December Just before Christmas the first copies of the *Idylls* with photographic illustrations by Mrs Cameron are published by Henry King. On the 29th, through Disraeli, the Queen once again offers T a baronetcy; he keeps to the decision he made with Gladstone.

1875

29 January Frederick Locker invites T to London; they could see the Old Masters together, smoke pipes in his den, and see Irving in *Hamlet*.

March T sees Henry Irving in *Hamlet*.

5 May Tom Hughes sends T some notes on dialect, some with reference to 'Wessex'.

7 May J. A. Froude, who has received an advance copy of *Queen Mary*, writes admiringly to T; it is 'the greatest' of all his works, and its anti-Papal theme has struck 'a more fatal blow than a thousand pamphleteers and controversialists'. (A second volume of the *Idylls* with new illustrations by Mrs Cameron appears during the month.)

June

3 (Thurs) T informs the Duchess of Argyll that 'Hallam has been at home all this Cambridge term and acting as secretary for us both – hard upon him I fear however good for us'.

23 Farrar writes to thank T for the copy of *Queen Mary*, which recalls his Freshwater visit, when he heard T read that 'noble drama'.

30 Browning writes to say that *Queen Mary* is 'astonishingly fine'; he is going 'to begin it afresh now'.

31 July T's 'Sir John Franklin', lines for his cenotaph in Westminster Abbey, appears in *The Times*.

Summer The Ts travel to Pau, where Emily, who has recovered sufficiently to make the journey, and has brought Locker's daughter Eleanor as her companion, stays with her and Lionel. They become engaged while Hallam and his father return to the western Pyrenees. On 20 August, Sir Henry Bedingfield, one of T's admirers, writes to him, expressing his surprise and pain on finding what an ignoble part had been assigned to his ancestor in *Queen Mary*.

3 October Mrs Procter, whose husband, the author 'Barry Cornwall', died in 1874, has stayed nine weeks at Beach House, Freshwater, disappointed from the first not to find the Ts at Farringford. She now writes to Lord Houghton, telling him that 'the last week has brought Mr Tennyson here, and we meet continually'.

Much of T's time in the winter months is taken up with difficulties arising in preparatory moves for the production of *Queen Mary* at the Lyceum Theatre. It needs to be reduced considerably, and much trouble arises over the incidental music, which he has asked one of Hallam's friends, Charles Villiers Stanford, to compose. The last of several objections raised by the management is that it demands so many musicians that two rows of stalls will have to be removed. Without telling Stanford, T offers to pay for all these seats. Somehow the problem is overcome without this loss, but T's generous offer is not forgotten by the young composer.

1876

February–March (or later) As in 1875, the Ts take a London house in February till Easter (each year to 1882), in order to be near Lionel while he works at the India Office, and also, as T said, to 'rub our country rust off' (cf. Hallam T, *Memoir* II, p. 222).

April

1 (Sat) Woolner hopes T will attend the Royal Academy banquet, 'the best thing of its kind'. 'To ramble about those grand rooms with Princes, and the greatest men in England smoking your pipe, as we all do, listening sometimes to exquisite glees and madrigals, is excellent fun. . . .'

15 T answers Sir H. Bedingfield's letter; he was abroad when it arrived, and has waited until the play is announced for acting. His ancestor's name will not be mentioned, and he has inserted a line in Elizabeth's part, 'Out, girl, you wrong a noble gentleman.' (Sir Henry was satisfied with this action.)

18 *Queen Mary* has its *première* at the Lyceum. Although many of his friends attend, T does not see the play until two weeks later. He is represented by Hallam, and Mrs Greville sends T an ecstatic report of it. (Its *succès d'estime* – as FitzGerald describes it – is brief; Henry Irving's role as Philip being short, and the play too shorn to do it justice, it is withdrawn in five weeks.)

19 Robert Browning writes, wishing to be among the earliest to assure T of 'the complete success' of his play.

25 Martin Tupper writes to congratulate T after seeing *Queen Mary* the previous evening. It is 'a wonderful reproduction of history living and moving and speaking before us'.

9 May In preparation for his next play, T visits with Hallam the battlefield where Harold was slain, and then writes, at Hastings, the poem 'Show-Day at Battle Abbey, 1876'.

21 June T, in London, reads the first draft of the last act of *Harold* to Palgrave, then takes P's children to the Zoological Gardens.

8 July The historian J. R. Green sends T the work he had promised, indicating where T's 'part of the story' begins. He cannot say how greatly he has enjoyed the previous two days at Aldworth.

21 July T's old friend R. C. Trench, Bishop of Dublin, replies to Hallam, after being consulted on the probability of the monks' singing 'such a hymn' (as in *Harold*).

September

T is too busy with *Harold* to take a long summer holiday. He and Hallam set out, probably in the second week, for a tour in Norfolk.

14 (Thurs) They call on Fitz at Woodbridge, Suffolk. As his house is being decorated, he finds accommodation for them at the Bull Inn.

15 They are all out for the day: by carriage to Ipswich, where they look at Wolsey Gate, then by steamer to Harwich and back, returning by carriage from Ipswich.

16 T and Hallam leave by train. Fitz and T had found that they could talk and joke as they had done 'twenty years ago' (cf. 1854).

October

2 (Mon) T's solicitor Arnold White meets Kegan Paul, Henry King's manager, on the question of issuing an annotated edition of his works. Reference to the contract shows that such a project is illegal without T's consent, and it is dropped. (King retires from the business later in the year.)

25 T informs Mrs Gladstone that he will come on Monday 'if all be well', and asks that he may smoke his pipe in his own room.

30 T's visit to Gladstone at Hawarden with Hallam begins; he reads the whole of *Harold* to the Gladstones.

31 Fitz writes to say that the Laurence portrait of T is packed and must go; he wishes Hallam to let him know whether it

is to be sent to Aldworth or Farringford. (Earlier they had wanted him to keep the picture.)

November *Harold,* dated 1877 and dedicated to Lord Lytton, son of Bulwer-Lytton (who had dedicated his novel *Harold* to T's uncle Charles) is published. Work on *Becket* has begun.

December

21 (Thurs) Louisa Ward writes from 21 Onslow Square to thank T for sending a copy of *Harold*. She thinks nothing can 'come up to the tragic force and passion of "Queen Mary" ', and hopes to receive him in London in February. Sophia Cracroft writes gratefully for her copy. She read it the first evening, she says, without leaving her chair, and has repeatedly turned to it with delight. She will now read Lytton's *Harold*.

28 Writing on 'the Feast of the Holy Innocents', Aubrey de Vere sends cordial thanks for *Harold,* in which he finds 'a sort of Aeschylean strength' throughout.

1877

13 January T is invited to attend the unveiling of the Burns statue in Glasgow on the 25th. (He is unable to attend.)

February The Ts probably move to London, where they have taken a house in Upper Wimpole Street. (See 17 Mar.)

March

T's prefatory sonnet 'Those that of late had fleeted far and fast' appears in the first number of *The Nineteenth Century,* founded by James Knowles after his resignation from the editorship of *The Contemporary Review*. T writes 'Montenegro', another sonnet, after discussing with Gladstone the bravery of this country against the Turks.

17 (Sat) T has taken a house in London for three months, Lord Houghton writes, but will dine out only at 7 p.m. (The Ts entertain a great deal, and form new friends, including Lord Selborne and the Hungarian violinist Joseph Joachim.)

24 T and Hallam meet the Leweses in the park, and take a long walk with them.

25 With Hallam and Lionel he calls on George Eliot at the Priory.

28 T and Hallam dine with Lord Houghton at Almond's Hotel to meet the archaeologist Heinrich Schliemann. T will not believe the latter's assertion that ancient Troy was no bigger than Burlington House courtyard. The guests include Gladstone and Henry James, who is disappointed that T does not appear 'Tennysonian', talking chiefly about port wine and tobacco.

30 As he had promised, T reads to a large party at the Priory, where Hallam has to stop him at midnight. ('It was a great success. Tennyson read "Maud" and the two "Northern Farmers" ', G. H. Lewes notes in his diary.)

16 April Tom Taylor has asked Chatto and Windus to send T a copy of his historical plays, and hopes to see him again, and have the pleasure of shaking hands with his wife.

23 April Lewes lunches with T, and is exasperated by Matilda T's 'nonsense and ignorance' on vivisection.

24 May Fitz has heard from Hallam T how much the Poet Laureate enjoyed his stay in London 'among all the Poets, Wits, and Philosophers'.

4 June Victor Hugo, who has met Lionel T in Paris and received T's sonnet addressed to him, writes to T, saying that France and England for him are one people.

6 July T and Hallam meet George Eliot and G. H. Lewes by chance, while the latter are on a drive from Witley Heights, their new country home.

August T and Hallam visit Canterbury to inspect 'each separate scene of Becket's martyrdom'.

25 September J. R. Green writes to say they will have great pleasure in coming to 'Haslemere' on Tuesday (2 Oct) for two nights before they leave for Italy.

October He visits Aldworth (most probably for the period indicated) and discusses *Becket* with T, who finds his intellect 'vivid as lightning'.

27 November Longfellow sends his sonnet 'Wapentake to Alfred Tennyson' as a Christmas greeting to T.

December This year, as remains their custom for some years, the Ts return to spend their Christmas–New Year season at Farringford.

1878

11 February Thoby Prinsep, who has been blind with cataract for several years, dies at the Briary.

25 February Lionel T and Eleanor Locker are married in Westminster Abbey. Dean Stanley, the bride's uncle, is too ill to officiate but blesses them in his bedroom. ET is carried to her seat in the Abbey by Hallam. A celebration for the servants and local residents takes place in the ballroom at Farringford.

March 'The Revenge' appears in *The Nineteenth Century*. (Afterwards T complained that 'the scoundrels only gave me £300 for that. It was worth £500!') On Sunday, the 31st, T and Hallam visit the Leweses at the Priory.

April

5 (Fri) T meets Lewes at Lord Houghton's tea.

8 Lewes and George Eliot lunch with the Ts. Knowles is another guest.

12 They dine with the Ts and meet Lord Acton with Annie (Thackeray) and her husband Richmond Ritchie. Later, before an enlarged company which includes the Cowper-Temples, Sir Garnet Wolseley, and Lord and Lady Monteagle, T reads 'The Revenge' and other of his poems. On the same day John Tyndall writes from Farringford, where he and his wife have been staying (at Hallam's suggestion). They expect to pass the Ts when they (the Tyndalls) return (to London).

17 Tyndall writes to say how much he and his wife Louisa

enjoyed their time at Farringford, and how regretful he is that the merchant who supplied the port he sent T did not tell him it required 'a month's rest' to be at its best.

May Mrs Cameron and her husband return to the Isle of Wight for a short visit from Ceylon, where they have been helping their sons to reorganize the family plantations.

June Locker forwards to Hallam T a request from Hubert von Herkomer to Dean Stanley for permission to take a portrait of T wherever the latter wishes. (The offer is accepted, and the sitting takes place at Farringford.)

12 July Arnold White informs T that Kegan Paul wishes to remain his publisher, but wonders if T will be in town next week to talk over the question.

Early summer Having made such good progress with *Becket* that he feels he can allow himself a longer holiday than he has taken since 1875, T visits Ireland with Hallam: Westport (Lord Sligo's), Galway, Mount Trenchard (Lord Monteagle's), the Shannon, Killarney, Dublin, and Wicklow.

12 August G. H. Lewes has lunch with the Ts at Aldworth, the only other guest being Mrs Greville. T seeks his professional view of *Becket* (not yet in its final form). L expresses some reservations, but conceals his more serious doubts.

22 August After lunch the Leweses bring Tom Trollope (the novelist's elder brother, who had settled in Italy) and his wife, who have never seen the poet. The visit proves 'most interesting'; T takes them to the spring, and reads them two of his new poems.

November Mrs Greville, after taking Henry James to see George Eliot at Witley Heights, brings him to luncheon at Aldworth. Afterwards, upstairs in the poet's study, he listens uncomfortably to T's low-pitched rendering of 'Locksley Hall'. On the 25th Arnold White informs ET that Kegan Paul accepts his stipulations, and hopes there will be no more difficulties with him.

3 December T sends 'our affectionate sympathies' (all, he says, that can be said at present) to George Eliot. (George Henry Lewes had died on 30 Nov.)

1879

January (early) Among the Farringford visitors for Christmas and the New Year the most eagerly expected must have been Lionel and Eleanor with their baby son (born 20 Nov and named Alfred Browning Stanley after his grandfather and his two godfathers.

31 January Mrs Greville leaves Farringford. She has recited 'The Grandmother' for one of Agnes Weld's charitable causes, and drawn tears from 'hundreds of eyes'. 'All the little girls' have been learning it since.

Early in the year T has trial sheets of *Becket* run off, and submits a copy to Irving, now manager of the Lyceum. Irving concludes that, even if it were considerably cut, the play would be too costly to produce.

February

14 (Fri) After difficult and very protracted negotiations, T's solicitor Arnold White reaches a legal publishing agreement with Kegan Paul, T being guaranteed £2500 p.a., the publishers accepting a 5 per cent commission on *Queen Mary*, *Harold*, and all his new works.

26 News has come of Mrs Cameron's death on 26 January, soon after her return to Ceylon. ET takes comfort in the thought that she enjoyed her visit to the Isle of Wight, and had such a happy week with her family just before her death.

27 G. M. Hopkins, writing to a friend, thinks that T ought to have called his *Idylls* 'Charades from the Middle Ages'.

(During their London season the Ts like to have Joachim play to their guests at 86 Eaton Square.)

March After collecting evidence from survivors and records, T writes 'The Defence of Lucknow', a dramatic account of long resistance by a 'handful' of British during the Indian Mutiny. In the 'Dedicatory Poem to the Princess Alice' which prefaces it (both published in the April issue of *The Nineteenth Century*) T makes plain why he dedicated the poem to her: she had died in December, as a result of kissing her child, who was ill with diphtheria.

20 March R. D. Adams writes from Sydney, Australia, wondering if T would like to compete for the prize of 100 guineas for a poem celebrating the forthcoming international exhibition in Sydney.

25 April T's brother Charles dies at Cheltenham. (His wife Louisa dies on 20 May.)

May

7 (Wed) After hearing that the first two parts of 'The Lover's Tale' (as printed in 1832) have been sold in a pirated edition (the work of R. H. Shepherd), one (the original perhaps) for £41, T decides to print the whole poem, including 'The Golden Supper'. (It appears before the end of the year.)

8 T is in 'a great rage' to hear of a review or notice of *Becket* under the title of 'Fair Rosamunde', and wonders if Irving has 'let the cat out of the bag'.

10 R. D. Adams informs T that his magnificent drama *Queen Mary* has been performed in Sydney for the first time, and sends a notice of it. His review of T's *Complete Poems* has led to a great demand for the volume at the library.

19 Spedding is expected at Farringford to help in arranging with T and Hallam the publication of Charles Turner's collected sonnets (an edition to which he contributes an analytical introduction; it appears in 1880, edited by Hallam).

T and Hallam spend 'two lovely May-days' with the historian W. E. H. Lecky, visiting Stonehenge, Salisbury Cathedral, Amesbury, George Herbert's church at Bemerton, and the Vandykes at Wilton.

30 June T writes 'Prefatory Poem to My Brother's Sonnets' late at night: its subtitle is 'Midnight, June 30, 1879'.

4 August His Spanish admirer, Vicente de Arana, sends him a copy of the *Revista Europea,* containing his article on T and his works, an introduction to an essay he proposes on *Idylls of the King*.

26 September T and Hallam call on George Eliot at Witley Heights (when she is feeling 'ill and depressed').

29 September T thanks his correspondent for a photograph of Longfellow's bust, and says that, having had his own done by Woolner, he has decided not to sit again to any sculptor, however excellent.

November He finishes *The Falcon,* a one-act dramatization of a story from Boccaccio's *Il Decamerone* (V, ix).

December (early) He has begun *The Cup,* a tragedy in two acts from Plutarch's *The Bravery of Women* (xx), suggested by a paragraph in Lecky's *History of European Morals.*

18 December The opening performance of *The Falcon* takes place at St James's Theatre, where it runs several weeks.

During December T contributes 'The City Child' and 'Minnie and Winnie', both 'rejected from *The Princess*', to the New York children's magazine *St Nicholas.* C. V. Stanford makes his acquaintance for the first time while staying at Farringford. T resigns from the Metaphysical Society.

1880

January T is provoked by John Churton Collins' article in *The Cornhill* on the echoes of classical poetry in his imagery. The intention, he assumes, is to cast doubt on his originality.

February T's two 'Child-Songs' appear in *St Nicholas.*

17 March He reads 'Camma' (*The Cup*) to Palgrave, who describes it as 'a piece powerfully written and very original'.

23 March Browning writes to Hallam from his home, 19 Warwick Crescent, saying that he will be happy to dine with them all on Easter Monday.

During March, Thomas Hardy, with Mrs Anne Procter, lunches at the Ts' in Belgrave Street. When he arrives ET is lying 'as if in a coffin', but she rises to welcome him and presides at the table in a reclining position. T is very sociable, 'asking Mrs Procter absurd riddles, and telling Hardy amusing stories, and about misprints in his books that drove him wild'. Students of Glasgow University invite him to accept nomination for the Lord Rectorship; he agrees to stand provided they represent their fellow students and not a political party.

7 May T declines to stand for the Rectorship when he learns that he is a Conservative party candidate. He had been led to believe that he was 'supported by a large majority if not a totality of the students'.

June As his father has not been well since the death of his brother Charles, Hallam acts on the advice of the physician Andrew Clark, and takes him to Venice. They travel via Munich (where they study picture galleries on the 13th and 14th), Tegernsee (staying at Lord Acton's), Innsbruck and the Dolomites, and Cortina, with a visit to the village where Titian was born. In Venice T is fascinated by the blaze of colour in sky and water, by St Mark's, the Doge's Palace, and Tintoretto's paintings.

July They return to Farringford (T much improved in health) by Verona, Lake Garda (with a special excursion to Sirmio, Catullus's peninsula, where, with Charles in mind, T composes 'Frater Ave atque Vale'), and Milan.

August

5 (Thurs) William Allingham and his wife Helen (*née* Paterson) walk from Haslemere to Aldworth, and are overtaken by T (who had called for them) in his carriage, with his grandson Alfred in his nurse's lap, and Mr Fields, his American publisher. On the lawn they find 'Mrs Tennyson lying horizontal in an invalid chair with a hood to it, wrapt in furs, and looking sadly pale and worn'.

8 Helen and WA walk up to Aldworth. T denounces vivisection 'most fiercely', and says his eyes are so weak he can read only half an hour at a time. He praises Arnold's 'The Scholar-Gipsy' and 'Thyrsis', and thinks 'Clive' the best poem in Browning's new volume.

11 T, 'with little Alfred and baby Charley', calls on the Allinghams at Haslemere, and has tea in the garden under an apple tree. (The Allinghams visit Aldworth on the 13th, 20th, and 29th.)

27 J. R. Lowell from the Legation of the United States in London writes, asking if T finds the proposed copyright treaty between the United States and Britain suitable.

September

2 (Thurs) T tells WA that Keats is wonderful, greater than Wordsworth, Coleridge, Byron, and Shelley (once an idol of his).

14 Cruising on the *Columba* near Oban, the Duke of Argyll writes to ET, and tells her how much they enjoyed their 'little visit'. He thinks the life, work, and death of St Columba a fitting subject for T, and almost sees another Idyll in it.

19 In a discussion with WA at Aldworth, T returns to the unreasonableness of the Irish, but (after referring to their 'horrible island') agrees that the English have been brutal and that the Celts are charming.

13 October He allows Helen to sketch him, and gives her an advance copy of Charles's sonnets.

21 October The Allinghams make their last visit to Aldworth this year; there is snow on the ground. T reads his poem 'The Voyage of Maeldune' (written with the Irish in mind from Joyce's *Old Celtic Romances*).

3 November He is pleased with Gladstone's appreciation of his brother's sonnets. 'He was almost the most lovable human being I have ever met', T writes. (A letter written later, when snow had fallen for the second time and the Ts were about to return to the Isle of Wight, shows how charmed he was with J. R. Lowell's 'brief, true, and delicate criticism' of Charles's sonnets. T thought he was 'a second George Herbert in his faith, without his ultra quaintness, and with as much, or, as it seems to me, more poetry in him than old Herbert had'.)

24 November Hallam and his father are 'just going off [from Aldworth] to read the new play to the Actors of the Lyceum Theatre'.

November (end) *Ballads and Other Poems* is published, with a dedicatory poem 'To Alfred Tennyson, My Grandson'. Its main inclusions are 'The First Quarrel', 'Rizpah', 'The Northern Cobbler', 'The Revenge', 'The Sisters', 'The Village Wife', 'The Children's Hospital', 'The Defence of Lucknow', 'Sir John Oldcastle, Lord Cobham', 'Columbus', and 'The Voyage of Maeldune'.

1881

3 January *The Cup* begins a four months' run at the Lyceum, with Ellen Terry and Henry Irving in the leading roles.

March (early) T, in London as had become his custom at this time of the year, hears of James Spedding's accident. He calls at St George's Hospital, where JS lies injured after being run over by a cab in Hill Street on 1 March, but is not allowed to see him. (Unlike Hallam, he fails to see him before his death on 9 March.)

20 (Sun) John Millais writes to T, suggesting the next three days for a sitting. (James Knowles has commissioned his portrait.)

22 Fitz writes to ET on JS's death, recalling his stay with T at Mirehouse (in 1835) when the daffodils were out.

23 Hallam and his father will be delighted to drive with Mrs William Smith on Friday. They leave London (9 Upper Belgrave Street) on the 6th.

12 May Millais informs Hallam that his father's portrait is the success that he hoped it would be.

5 June Coventry Patmore writes on the apparent breakdown of friendly relations between him and the Ts. Their assumption that he needed assistance (cf. July 1862) had vexed him. He had invited T to see him, and had received no reply.

11 June Patmore is reassured by T's answer to his letter.

(During June the Allinghams move to Sandhills, Witley.)

7 July Eleanor T and her two children are at Farringford.

25 July Mrs Procter sends T one of Hardy's novels (probably *The Trumpet-Major*, published Oct 1880). The people in it, she says, are not exalted, but good simple souls; and the heroine marries the wrong man. (She thought the heroine like herself when she was young, and signed herself 'Anne Loveday' when she wrote to Hardy, who had her in mind when he described Anne at the opening of the novel.)

21 August During the Allinghams' visit to Aldworth T reveals that the name of the original for the farmer in his 'proputty' poem ('Northern Farmer, New Style') was Thimbleby. His wife used to say, 'The day I married Thimbleby I brought him £5000 on each shoulder!'

October (?) T and Hallam visit Newstead Abbey (Byron's home) and Sherwood Forest. (He is writing *The Foresters*, another full-length play – first produced in March 1892, by Augustin Daly in New York, before its publication in London.)

November 'Despair', published in *The Nineteenth Century*, provokes much criticism, many readers failing to realize the implications of its subtitle 'A Dramatic Monologue'.

16 December Gladstone writes to say that he is sorry the vacancy in his office has been filled, but perhaps another will occur for Hallam. He would think himself fortunate to have him as his assistant.

1882

13 January T, in his study at Aldworth, cannot bear to be sketched, or stared at, by Helen Allingham.

2 February Tyndall invites T, who has 'sung of Lucretius and of Atoms', to come and hear something more about them at

9 o'clock; he can offer dinner at 7, with the best wine his merchant can find. (The year is conjectural.)

During February, while in London, at 86 Eaton Square, T turns his 1852 'Hands All Round!' into a patriotic song, which ET sets to music (arranged by C. V. Stanford) for Queen Victoria's birthday.

March 'The Charge of the Heavy Brigade at Balaclava' appears in *Macmillan's Magazine*.

10 March Hallam informs Mrs W. Smith that his father will be delighted to drive with her tomorrow at four o'clock (Sat).

Spring At Farringford the Ts entertain Sir Henry Parkes, Premier of New South Wales. T meets Mary Boyle at the Briary, where Lord and Lady Kenmare are staying.

18 May From Wellington College, Wokingham, the Revd E. C. Wickham sends T a copy of Horace's Odes 'to replace the gondoliers' handywork' (cf. June 1880). To have been T's travelling-companion is his 'greatest literary honour'. He hopes too that the book will be regarded as an expression of gratitude for T's kindness and 'true hospitality' last month.

6 July T's friend W. G. Ward dies (cf. his poem 'In Memoriam W. G. Ward'). With the death of his brother Charles in 1879, and of Carlyle, Spedding, Drummond Rawnsley, and Dean Stanley in 1881, few of his old friends are left, and he feels disconsolate.

August
With Hallam he enjoys a few days in Derbyshire.

9 (Wed) After driving from Ashbourne to Ilam, they take rooms at the Izaak Walton Hotel and explore Dovedale.

10 They walk along the Manifold valley to Ilam Hall, then stroll up Dovedale again.

11 They drive over the hills to Hartington, then walk to Hall Dale and Beresford Dale, finding the latter a contrast to Mill Dale, which is 'sinuous, spacious and bare'.

13 They return to Aldworth, highly delighted with the uniqueness of Dovedale.

18 Cardinal Newman writes to say that, owing to the infirmities of old age, he must decline the invitation from the Ts which he has received through Aubrey de Vere.

September 'To Virgil', written in response to a request from Mantua (dated 23 June and acknowledged on 10 Sep) for the nineteenth centenary of Virgil's death, appears in *The Nineteenth Century*.

11 November T's new drama *The Promise of May* is produced at the Globe, after being refused by Irving. (It creates a storm among freethinkers, and is withdrawn after five weeks.)

December (early) Annie Ritchie is at Aldworth with T and his 'party'. All is well and merry, she informs Fitz, despite the fiasco of T's pastoral play. (Whether this is her addition, or Fitz's when reporting to Frederick T on 14 Jan 1883, is not clear.)

1883

March T writes letters of sympathy to Queen Victoria on her fall, and on the death of her personal attendant John Brown. He has been advised not to stay in London as early this year, lest the fogs should cause a recurrence of his gout.

6 April The Ts are still at Farringford. They have had Lady Sophia Palmer and Lady Ashburton and her daughter as their guests, and others before them.

April (later) While staying with Granville Bradley, Stanley's successor as Dean of Westminster, T is invited by the Archdeacon, F. W. Farrar, to write lines, turning on *Fiat Lux*, for a memorial window to Caxton (the gift of London printers) in St Margaret's (cf. 'Epitaph on Caxton', which F acknowledged on 7 May). Gladstone meets T at the Deanery, where they discuss the Irish question. T sees Ellen Terry in *Much Ado About Nothing* at the Lyceum.

6 May Writing to Sir Henry Ponsonby, T thanks the Queen for her kind words, but regrets that since his return from town he has not been well enough to undertake so long a drive against the east wind, or he would come to see her at Osborne.

14 June Edward FitzGerald dies.

17 June T writes to Pollock, telling him he has written a dedicatory poem to Fitz 'within the last week'. (This prologue to 'Tiresias', to which he added an epilogue before its publication, recalls T's Woodbridge visit in 1876, and pays tribute to FitzGerald's *Rubáiyát*.)

August

7 (Tues) In response to the request of the Queen, who has been reading *In Memoriam* again, T visits Osborne from Aldworth, and spends an hour with her in Prince Albert's room. She notices his poor eyesight, and thinks he is 'very shaky on his legs'.

25 Palgrave visits T at Aldworth.

26 He has a 'longish' walk with him, and hears him read 'Tiresias'.

27 T has been finishing and revising 'Tiresias' (much of which was written in 1833).

September

8 (Sat) Hallam and T are guests with the Gladstones on the trial cruise of Sir Donald Currie's ship *The Pembroke Castle*. They embark at Barrow and anchor off the Isle of Man. (Their course lies round western Scotland, stopping at a number of points, including Tobermory, where Sir Andrew Clark comes on board with his wife and daughter. From Kirkwall they have a smooth crossing to Kristiansand, in southern Norway, and again to Copenhagen, where they visit the Thorwaldsen Museum.)

17 Hallam is one of the many notabilities who dine with the King and Queen of Denmark at the Castle of Fredensborg. T does not attend.

18 Royalty lunches on board *The Pembroke Castle*. Gladstone proposes the health of the King of Denmark; the Tsar, the health of Queen Victoria; and the Queen of Denmark, that of T. At the request of the Princess of Wales, T reads

'The Bugle Song' ('The splendour falls on castle walls', at the end of *The Princess*, III) and 'The Grandmother' in the smoking-room. The ship leaves at four o'clock to the cheers of the sailors on English, French, Russian, and Danish battleships.

19 Gravesend is reached in the morning. (During the voyage Hallam, unaware that his father has re-opened the question through an intermediary, is asked by Gladstone whether he thinks T would accept a peerage.)

24 T writes to Mary Boyle, and tells her that he has just met queens and princesses, but none 'more royal in her sweetness and noble innocence than my own dear Audrey' (her niece). 'I verily believe that the better heart of me beats stronger at 74 than ever it did at 18', he adds. (An engagement between Hallam T and Audrey Boyle is announced in the latter part of the year. She had stayed with her aunt Mary at Freshwater, and visited Farringford, in the spring.)

27 ET's reply to Gladstone makes it clear that the offer he has intimated will be accepted; she is grateful that Hallam will inherit 'the duties belonging to this distinction'.

6 October T is not well enough to write. Emily thanks Gladstone for his goodness and the telegram and all he has done connected with the peerage.

November Frederick Locker and Sir Edward Hamley visit T at Aldworth, and discuss the charge of the Heavy Brigade at Balaclava, and T's poem on the subject (cf. the prologue to this poem). Gladstone mentions the possibility of having Arthur Hallam's letters to him published by Knowles in *The Nineteenth Century* (after the publication of those to Milnes Gaskell), but T opposes the suggestion; the letters should at least be submitted to him. On the 25th Louisa Tyndall writes, hoping Hallam can persuade his parents to lunch with them at Hindhead on Wednesday (the 28th).

December T asks Gladstone if he may assume the name of Tennyson d'Eyncourt; if the younger branch of his family can claim such lineage, he can. Emily being too weak to travel, the Ts remain at Aldworth (and stay for the whole of the winter).

1884

15 January T begins a ten-year contract with Macmillan and Co. He is to receive one-third of the advertised price on all books sold, with an annual advance of £1500, which is guaranteed should the royalty any year fail to reach this sum.

February
The Cup and *The Falcon* are published in one volume.
13 (Wed) He receives from the Queen a copy of her *More Leaves from a Journal of our Life in the Highlands* inscribed 'To her Poet Laureate'.
26 W. H. Thompson thanks T for the copy of *The Cup and The Falcon* he has sent. The second play is 'particularly excellent', and the Great Council of the Nation is to be congratulated on numbering T among its members.

March
Writing from Farringford for his father, who is 'suffering from his eyes', Hallam informs J. Dykes Campbell that T is sorry his sonnet 'Lines on Cambridge of 1830' ('Therefore your Halls, your ancient Colleges') has been reprinted. He has a great affection for his old university, and regrets that 'this spirit of undergraduate irritability against the then state of things ever found its way into print'.
11 (Tues) T, who is staying with the Bradleys at the Deanery of Westminster, takes his seat in the House of Lords, where he is introduced by the Duke of Argyll and Lord Kenmare (deputizing for Lord Houghton, who is in Greece).
29 On hearing of the death of the Queen's youngest son, the Duke of Albany, T writes and sends her the epitaph 'Prince Leopold'.

17 April As part of the tercentenary celebrations at the University of Edinburgh, the honorary degree of Doctor of Laws (LL.D.) is bestowed on Robert Browning, and on T *in absentia*.

About this time or a little later H. D. Rawnsley (Drummond's son) makes his first visit to Farringford, and finds the poet working on his 'Epitaph on Lord Stratford de Redcliffe' for the statue which is to be unveiled in Westminster Abbey on 24 May. It is the sort of thing he says he hates doing. The only epitaph that completely satisfied him, he tells Rawnsley, is the one he wrote on Sir John Franklin (R's great-uncle).

25 June Hallam T and Audrey Boyle are married in the Henry VII Chapel, Westminster Abbey. T enters with Mrs Locker; Emily, in a bath-chair, her dress being taken care of by Lionel. A most distinguished gathering includes Lord Houghton, Browning, Lecky, Matthew Arnold, old Mrs Procter, and the Allinghams. After the ceremony the Ts and their many guests are entertained at the Deanery.

27 June ET is too ill to travel from Aldworth to Farringford.

July T writes to Gladstone on 'matter of justice', the extension of the franchise. 'The nation is one and includes all ranks of people', he holds. Hallam and his wife Audrey are to be domiciled at Farringford, he being indispensable to both his father and his mother. On the 26th Allingham spends the afternoon at Aldworth, and helps T with the Irish brogue of 'Molly Magee' (later entitled 'Tomorrow'), a subject provided by Aubrey de Vere, its language being drawn to some extent from Carleton's *Traits of the Irish Peasantry*.

7 August The Allinghams visit Aldworth. T tells WA that he sees most magnificent landscapes in dreams, and on closing his eyes. He has red *Fleurs du Mal*, and (unlike WA) thinks Baudelaire 'a kind of moralist'.

8 September At Aldworth the Allinghams see T blowing bubbles to amuse Lionel's boys.

24 September After he and his second wife have stayed with the Ts, Frederick Locker writes from Rowfant, Crawley, Sussex (his father-in-law's house), hoping that T can stay with them, bringing Emily if possible. (T and Hallam accept the invitation. Their host takes the name of Locker-Lampson in 1885, adding his wife's family name to his own.)

November

6 (Thurs) At Aldworth with the naturalist Alfred Wallace, the Allinghams find T unwell and rather sad. W speaks

on behalf of spiritualism, and T suggests that 'the Unseen World' is 'a great ocean pressing round us on every side, and only leaking in by a few chinks'.

14 T sends his 'Compromise' to Gladstone. This poem of advice during a period of agitation about the Franchise Bill had appeared, without authorization apparently, in the *St James's Gazette* on 29 October.

25 WA walks up to Aldworth, and stays for the night. Matilda T is present, and Miss Ritchie arrives from London. She plays some Beethoven and, at Hallam's request, Edward FitzGerald's 'Locksley Hall' music, which she finds structurally amateurish. WA judges that T 'is very fond of Gladstone as a private friend'.

26 Matilda reminds T of the stories he used to tell his brothers and sisters at Somersby; 'The Old Horse' lasted for months.

5 December WA takes Helen to sketch on Blackdown. She is so cold that they decide to call at Aldworth for a cup of tea. On the way they meet T. He has 'always felt that there must be *Some one who knows* – that is, *God*. But I am in hopes that I shall find something human in Him too.' Lady T, 'a dear, almost angelic woman', comes down to dinner, very pale; she has to be almost carried upstairs by Hallam.

8 December T thanks Paul Hayne for his present of North Carolina tobacco.

During December *Becket*, dedicated to Lord Selborne, the Chancellor, is published.

The year has seen the publication of T's collected poems in seven volumes, and in a single volume, for both of which editions T has revised carefully.

1885

10 January Palgrave, on a visit to Aldworth, finds Jowett there. (One evening, he notes, T read several recent 'poems in his ballad style'; P found 'extraordinary power and beauty' in them.)

12 January The musician Stanford arrives.

23 April (St George's Day) 'The Fleet' is published in *The Times*. T has been roused to write this by articles in *The Pall Mall Gazette* on the weakness of the British navy.

28 April Hallam T invites (successfully) Cardinal Manning to serve on the committee (of which T is a member) for the founding, at Aldershot, of a Gordon Cadet Corps for poor boys, in accordance with General Gordon's wish. (Gordon had been killed in January at Khartoum. The result of the committee's deliberations was the establishment of the Gordon Boys' Home for homeless and destitute boys.)

7 May T's epitaph on General Gordon (written at the request of the American poet Whittier) is published in *The Times*.

28 June Palgrave presents a copy of his *Selection of Lyrical Poems by Lord Tennyson* (with its affectionate dedication) to Lady Tennyson.

July

1 (Wed) From Farringford T informs the industrious literary editor A. B. Grosart that he knows 'absolutely nothing' about Henry Vaughan except his poem 'They are all gone into the world of light'.

9 He sends a copy of 'To H.R.H. Princess Beatrice' to the Queen, but begs to be excused from attending the wedding: he is too short-sighted.

12 Queen Victoria writes, indicating her wish that T discover whether Gladstone is willing to retire.

23 T's poem in honour of Princess Beatrice's marriage to Prince Henry of Battenburg appears in *The Times*.

9 August He writes to thank the Queen for her birthday congratulations.

During August Hallam and he stay at Gavelacre (lent them by Stewart Hodgson), on an island in the river Test near Andover in Hampshire.

21 September Sir Alfred Lyall, Lieutenant-Governor of the North-West provinces of India, thanks T for his autographed photograph, which has been forwarded.

October

1 (Thurs) T is made an offer of $50,000 for fifty readings on a tour of the United States. (He declines, as he had done similar offers in 1861 and 1863.)

6 Lionel leaves Aldworth for India at the invitation of Lord Dufferin. He wishes to see as much of the country as possible to further his work in the India Office. Eleanor accompanies him, their children staying with their aunt, Lady Frances Baillie, in Scotland.

13 WA goes to Aldworth; he has been reading Trollope. T considers his novels dull and prosaic, with 'never a touch of poetry'. They talk of Lyme Regis, William Barnes, and the kindliness of Lord Houghton (who had died at Vichy in August).

November

6 (Fri) WA walks from Sandhills through Haslemere to Aldworth.

7 He recommends General Gordon's *Journals*, which T has not read. T makes light of the 'stercoraceous qualities' of Rabelais, and recalls reading him aloud to friends at Cambridge, who nearly fell off their chairs for laughing. His foulness was but a mask for his free-thought.

13 After lunch at Aldworth, the Allinghams are taken down the new road to the Weald, where T shows them an old ruinous cottage, which Helen sketches.

December

Tiresias and Other Poems is published. Among the 'Other Poems' are 'Frater Ave atque Vale', 'To Virgil', 'The Charge of the Heavy Brigade', 'Despair', 'The Spinster's Sweet-Arts', 'Tomorrow', 'The Wreck', 'The Ancient Sage', and 'Balin and Balan' (a final contribution to *Idylls of the King*, giving the whole, in twelve parts, when it appeared in the New Library Edition of 1888, an epic appearance).

12 (Sat) T thanks Bosworth Smith for the collected letters he has sent on the Disestablishment question, and agrees with him

that the disestablishment and disendowment of the Church would mean the loss of 'much that is greatest and best' in England.

19 Viscount Wolseley thanks T for the honour he has done him by sending a copy of his latest book of poems.

1886

January (mid) Lionel is stricken with fever while hunting in Assam.

17 February Fearing he is unwell, Hallam writes to Edward Lear. He will go to see his pictures when they reach England, and asks if he can assist in getting them engraved and published.

11 March Lear's picture for ET and Hallam has just been unpacked. This 'magnificent' present is to be hung at Aldworth, Hallam informs Lear.

April

By the early part of this month Lionel has recovered sufficiently from his operation, it is thought, to undertake the voyage home. From Calcultta he is accompanied by Eleanor and a doctor who is returning to England.

16 (Fri) On hearing of Lionel's critical illness, the Queen sends a message of sympathy to the Ts and to 'poor little Eleanor', whom she has known from her (Eleanor's) earliest childhood.

20 He dies on his return voyage, and his body is committed to the Red Sea (cf. T's poem 'To the Marquis of Dufferin and Ava'). (Eleanor has kept his parents informed by telegram.)

25 The Queen sends her deepest sympathy to the Ts.

4 May T's 'Opening of the Indian and Colonial Exhibition by the Queen', written at the request of the Prince of Wales, is sung at the Albert Hall to the music of Sir Arthur Sullivan.

June Dr Oliver Wendell Holmes and his daughter visit the Ts at Farringford. The Ts return to Aldworth.

July T and Hallam see Lady Archibald Campbell and her company perform scenes from *Becket* in the Canizzaro Wood at Wimbledon. They stay with the Knowleses (now at Queen Anne's Lodge, St James's Park), visit the Colonial Exhibition, and see *Faust* at the Lyceum. After lunching with the Tyndalls at the Royal Institution, they proceed to Cromer, where they are the guests of the Locker-Lampsons.

August

7 (Sat) After various Norfolk excursions and sailing on Wroxham Broad, they reach Cambridge, where T lodges at Trinity. They dine with the University librarian.

8 They dine with Aldis Wright, Vice-Master of Trinity, and the conversation turns to Shakespeare and Jane Austen.

21 Merivale sends his regrets that he was absent from his deanery (at Ely) a week or two previously when T and Hallam called. He is shocked to think how much they have lost sight of each other 'since the days when we reciprocated poetry and puns among so many congenial spirits'.

About this time, and later perhaps, guests at Aldworth include Canon Ainger, Sir Andrew and Lady Clark, and Lord Napier of Magdala, who had been honoured for his bravery in the relief of Lucknow (Sep 1857), a subject T discusses with him; Napier thinks that T's poem 'The Defence of Lucknow' gives the impression that its author had been present during the siege.

27 Allingham finds T conversing with Dr Grailey Hewitt; T looks fine, 'grandly simple, gently dignified'.

27 October At Aldworth T reads 'Locksley Hall Sixty Years After' to Palgrave.

31 (?) October T tells WA that he never appreciated Horace until he was forty.

November Palgrave finds T at Aldworth 'unbroken in strength and mind', though 'depressed by the state of England and his own loss'. On the 24th he speaks gloomily, not for the first time, about England's future and the possibility of war. WA says it could be avoided by withdrawing from India. 'We are doing everything possible for them in India, and they roar and rage against us', T replies.

December
Locksley Hall Sixty Years After, a volume which includes *The Promise of May*, is published.

13 (Mon) Montagu Butler, who has just been appointed Master of Trinity, Cambridge, visits Farringford, staying until the 15th.

14 F. W. Farrar writes to thank T for his new volume of poems: 'sad, with a noble and inevitable sadness, and the great Eternal Hope gleams behind the gathering clouds'.

22 Sir Henry Thompson writes, expressing his appreciation of T's kindness in sending him an autographed copy of the *Locksley Hall* volume.

1887

13 January T receives an old tankard from the Cock Tavern, Fleet Street, in recognition of his 'Will Waterproof' poem (written half a century earlier).

15 January T sends thanks to Walt Whitman for 'A Word about Tennyson' in *The Critic*, and New Year greetings on the wings of the east wind, which he trusts is blowing more softly and warmly on his head than at Farringford, where it is rocking the elms and ilexes in the garden.

During January 'The Revenge' is sung to Stanford's setting in the Albert Hall, and an article by Gladstone on reforms achieved since 1842 (when 'Locksley Hall' was published) appears in *The Nineteenth Century* to answer the pessimism of 'Locksley Hall Sixty Years After'. It concludes: 'Justice does not require, nay rather she forbids, that the Jubilee of the Queen be marred by tragic notes.'

February T completes 'On the Jubilee of Queen Victoria' (begun the previous December).

12 March T thanks the Queen for her kind letter, and for communications concerning royalty in Russia. ('Rarely indeed have the tragic scenes of perfidy, cruelty and baseness, which they so touchingly relate been equalled', he writes.) She may feel lonely in the midst of rejoicing, but the dead may be more living than the living, and her lost husband, daughter, and son may rejoice when they hear the people shout the name of their queen.

11 May The Jubilee ode, set to Stanford's music, and conducted by him, is performed at Buckingham Palace. (During the month T finishes 'Demeter and Persephone'.)

July (? starting late June) T, with Hallam and his wife Audrey, cruises in *The Stella*, Sir Allen Young's yacht, for two weeks or more, enjoying calm waters and glorious sunshine. They sail to Dartmouth, round by the shores of Lyonnesse to Lundy Island and the south-west coast of Wales (with a visit to St David's Cathedral), then to Ilfracombe and Clovelly. After landing at Tintagel, and stopping at Falmouth, Fowey, and Plymouth, they cross to Guernsey and Jersey, where they visit Frederick T at his home near St Helier. (The two brothers talk of Somersby, tilting and tourneys in the fields there, the waste shore at Mablethorpe, college friends, old age, and spiritualism, in which F is a firm believer.) After exploring Alderney and calling at Cherbourg, they proceed to Freshwater Bay.

August R. C. Jebb, who, after being a fellow of Trinity College, Cambridge, succeeded Edmund Lushington as Professor of Greek at Glasgow, is the Ts' guest at Aldworth. He and T watch the eclipse of the moon from the sitting-room window balcony. The American actress Mary Anderson (then performing in *The Winter's Tale* in London) pays a visit, and signs an agreement to produce *The Cup*.

September

11 (Sun) WA drives with his wife Helen to Aldworth, where Viscount Wolseley appears with his daughter (after walking up from Manor House, Haslemere), and talks about the Nile and a mummy of 'the Pharoah, the friend of Moses'.

12 Frederick Bailey writes from Canterbury on the comfort

he receives from T's poetry. His wife and he have two children, both deaf and dumb; she encourages him to take down T's poems and read to her until he is 'strengthened and comforted'.

15 The Allinghams meet Arthur T and his wife at Aldworth. T finishes 'The Ring'.

22 After being brought to Aldworth by Alexander Macmillan from Liphook, William Gifford Palgrave writes to thank T for seeing him again on his 'flying visit'. He has asked Macmillan to send T a copy of *Ulysses*, a collection of travel essays which he expects to be published in November if not sooner.

31 October Sir Edwin Arnold sends T a copy of his latest volume of verse as a token of his admiration for T's works.

November

T and Hallam visit Cambridge to see *Oedipus Tyrannus* in Greek and *The Winter's Tale*.

15 (Tues) T writes to Walt Whitman, acknowledging the receipt of his photograph. England can learn something from the American Constitution, especially from the care of Americans to guard it from 'rash and unwise innovators'.

25 At Aldworth the Allinghams find T, in a red woollen cape, reading at a window. He 'praises the picturesqueness of the great fens, and the sun rising over the eastern sea'.

December

15 (Thurs) 'Owd Roä' is ready for the press.

30 Hallam T gives readings in the Freshwater assembly-hall of his father's poems 'The First Quarrel' and 'The Northern Cobbler'.

31 'Ally' and Charlie (Lionel's boys) 'seem to have had a very merry Christmas', ET informs her sister Anne.

1888

14 February At Farringford T reads the Wellington ode and 'The Spinster's Sweet-Arts' to his distinguished visitors Princess Beatrice, Prince Henry of Battenburg, and Sir Henry Ponsonby.

15 February T writes to Princess Beatrice, after her memorable visit yesterday, to thank her for the photograph of the Queen – the Jubilee year memorial – which she left. It had not been opened until after her departure.

1 April Mary Anderson is staying at Farringford. (During this Easter break she hears T read 'The Leper's Bride', which he has just finished; it is published with 'Happy' as its main title.)

18 April T writes to Charles Esmarch, objecting to the statement that he (T) is the hero of 'Locksley Hall Sixty Years After'. *'There is not one touch of autobiography in it from beginning to end'*, though some of his thought may be expressed in it. 'The whole thing is a dramatic impersonation.'

June Mary Anderson comes to discuss a production of *The Foresters*. On the 18th she is taken to the New Forest. At Lyndhurst they are joined by Lionel's two boys, who have been brought from a neighbouring school by the master, Drummond Rawnsley's son Willingham, much to T's delight.

July The Ts move to Aldworth (where their summer guests include Boyd Carpenter, Aubrey de Vere, Franklin Lushington, the Duke of Argyll, and Lord Carnarvon).

5 August Edmund Gosse walks from his sister-in-law's at Marley to have tea at Aldworth, where he meets Aldis Wright. After being taken round the grounds and house, he leaves, waving goodbye to T, a 'strange old piratical figure . . . in black . . . like a sort of vision of a superannuated highwayman'.

During August Hallam takes T to Chichester, then to Kingly Vale, to see the grove of trees sketched by Edward Lear (who died the previous January at his home in San Remo) for 'The Ballad of Oriana'.

1 September Allingham goes to Aldworth, and finds T about to leave for the station, where he meets Mary Anderson, who comes to discuss acting in *The Cup* in Birmingham and Dublin.

9 September While walking in the country with Sir Alfred Lyall, T notices the swelling of his knees. (Within a week he is very ill with gout and rheumatic fever. Sir Andrew Clark attends him three times from London; and Dr Dabbs, several times from the Isle of Wight.)

Early autumn T's old friend George Venables comes to Aldworth for the last time.

November

1 (Thurs) Hearing from Hallam that his father would like to see him, Palgrave arrives. T repeats emphatically 'his constant estimate of Wordsworth as the greatest of our poets in this century'. (During this visit he reads 'To Ulysses', his poem in commendation of *Ulysses* by Palgrave's brother Gifford, who has very recently died.)

3 On his way to Aldworth, Allingham meets Mrs T (Hallam's wife probably) driving Palgrave to the station. He finds T lying back, lean and pale, in his study.

15 John Tyndall writes to Hallam from Hind Head House, Haslemere. He and his wife had called at Aldworth at the end of October, on the first day of their holiday, and had crept away when they heard that T had fallen asleep, and Emily and Hallam were with him. He has heard 'words of cheer' from Dr Whiting, and hopes for confirmation on Sunday.

21 T is removed to Farringford.

December He has a serious relapse. On the 26th ET replies for him to Lord Napier of Magdala, who had been Commander-in-Chief in India, and who had just sent his Christmas good wishes, with the hope that the pen which has never failed to call on England's greatness in the time of need will 'flourish for many years to come'.

1889

January Browning, just home from Venice, wishes to know how T is. Jowett spends much time in conversation with T, who is carried down for the first time, to the drawing-room, on the 27th.

February In an interval between attacks he writes 'By an Evolutionist'.

9 March He goes out for the first time since his return to Farringford.

21 March He is able to see Lady Rosebery, who lunches with the Ts, and he praises her husband's 'feeling for the empire'.

17 April Gleams of sunshine entice him to the summer-house in Maiden's Croft. (About this time Montagu Butler, on a flying visit to Freshwater with his second wife, pays T a visit. They discuss Euripides, and the lack of sympathy between dons and undergraduates when T was at Trinity.)

May
In the middle of the month Sir Andrew Clark pronounces T fully recovered.
21 (Tues) T and Hallam leave for a cruise with Andrew Hichens and his wife (a niece of Thoby Prinsep) to Dartmouth, Plymouth, and Salcombe on Lord Brassey's yacht *The Sunbeam*. (While at Salcombe he visits J. A. Froude at the Moult, the late Earl of Devon's residence.)
26 The poem 'Parnassus', which T had extended and revised earlier in the year, may have been completed on this day.
28 H. G. Bohn sends him a copy of the new edition of his *Dictionary of Poetical Quotations*. He feels it is a 'literary duty' to do so; it contains alterations to the edition he gave T some fourteen years ago.

June
2 (Sun) Hallam writes to his mother from Portland.
4 A telegram indicates that T and Hallam expect to return via Yarmouth in the evening.
17 T thanks Gladstone for his kind message.

22 July Browning's attack on FitzGerald in *The Athenaeum* (after reading in Aldis Wright's edition of his letters Fitz's remark to W. H. Thompson, in his letter of 15 July 1861, 'Mrs Browning's Death is rather a relief . . . no more Aurora Leighs, thank God!') causes T to ask Emily to tell him 'with his love that Fitz never meant what you have him to mean'. 'We grieve deeply for you and your son and FitzGerald's family', she writes.

6 August The many congratulations T receives on his eightieth birthday include tributes from Browning, Swinburne, Theodore Watts-Dunton, Alfred Austin, Sir Henry Parkes in Australia, and W. E. H. Lecky. Louisa Ward wishes she could tell him how much she owes him, and Mrs Granville Bradley reminds him that it is exactly thirty-four years ago since the Ts came to see them at Alum Bay.

9 August The Queen sends her best wishes for T's birthday. She had not forgotten it, but her time had been taken up with the visit of her grandson, the Emperor of Germany.

At 8.15 one morning about this time Cecil Spring Rice looks out of his window at Aldworth and sees 'the bard running in the sun'. During the month T writes 'Merlin and the Gleam'.)

8 September He is annoyed at the omission of words from 'The Throstle' in *The New Review*; 'I think there never was a short poem so abominably abused.' (He believed that Gosse, who had asked him 'to let him have' a poem for *The New Review*, had sent the editor an imperfect copy.)

October Alfred Austin (who became Poet Laureate in 1896) visits T. 'Crossing the Bar' occurs to the latter while crossing the Solent on his way to Farringford; he shows a copy of it to Hallam after dinner the same day.

7 November Lionel Hallam T, son of Hallam and Audrey, is born. (He became famous as a cricketer, playing in Test Matches for England.)

December

12 (Thurs) Robert Browning dies in Venice. T's *Demeter and Other Poems* is published. (It contains some excellent short poems in addition to 'Demeter and Persephone','Owd Roä', 'The Ring', 'Happy', 'Merlin and the Gleam', and 'Romney's Remorse'; 20,000 copies are sold in the first week.)

24(?) T. H. Huxley writes to thank T for his copy of *Demeter*; he has not had a Christmas box he values so much for many a year.

31 Browning is buried in Westminster Abbey, and Hallam T takes his father's place as pall-bearer.

1890

10 January Herbert Warren, President of Magdalen College, Oxford, writes to T on the pleasure he has derived from T's works, and from seeing the younger generation of students enjoy *Demeter* and other T poems.

Early in the year T is suddenly stricken with bronchial pneumonia, from which he is slow to recover.

1 February T receives from J. Cuming Walters a copy of his book *In Tennyson Land*. Replying for his father, Hallam thanks him for the book, but wishes he had not ridden his hobby to death by identifying so much in his poems with Lincolnshire.

February (early) In response to Princess Beatrice's invitation, T sends the lines 'Remembering him who waits thee far away' for inscription in the prayer-book given to the Queen by her children at Osborne on the fiftieth anniversary of her wedding (on the 10th).

28 February Mary Anderson writes from Mentone to tell T that she is engaged to marry Fernando de Navarro.

March

8 (Sat) At his father's request Hallam reads him Robert Southwell's 'The Burning Babe' from Palgrave's *Treasury of Sacred Song*.

11 T recalls addressing boys at Louth Grammar School, in a long and comic speech, as if he were his uncle Charles, M.P. for Stamford; he hated the school so much that, in later life, he wouldn't go down the lane where it stood.

16 He talks of Lionel, this being his birthday, and thinks of *The Messiah*, *The Pilgrim's Progress*, and *Paradise Lost*, which are for him the three greatest religious works produced in England.

17 All but recovered from his influenza, he sits in the sun in front of his study window reading Jebb's *Homer*, an introduction to the *Iliad* and the *Odyssey*.

27 Writing from Cambridge, Massachusetts, J. R. Lowell says that he had been about to thank T for the honour of linking his (Lowell's) name with one of his poems ('The Ring') when he was taken seriously ill. Now recovered, he tells T that the *Demeter* volume is 'a wonder' to him, 'showing you so nobly undiminished in every way'.

28 Montagu Butler and his wife have tea at Farringford. T says 'Crossing the Bar' came to him in five minutes, adding, 'Anyhow, under ten minutes'.

April News comes that Mary Anderson is to be married, and will therefore be unable to act in *The Foresters*. Audrey T observes that T is still 'maddened' by the identification of Lincolnshire places with scenes in his poems, and by the assumption that poets have no creative imagination.

30 April Robert Bridges sends T a copy of his recent play.

15 May The gift of a phonograph having been sent from Thomas Edison, and its use demonstrated, T records some of his poems, including 'The Charge of the Light Brigade'. (During the month H. D. Rawnsley pays a visit to T, who tells him that Emily has been his 'life-long and truest critic'.)

28 May G. F. Watts leaves after completing a portrait of T for Trinity College. T recalls acting in Dryden's plays with his brothers and sisters, and the assurance of the French governess that he would be a fine actor some day.

June

13 (Fri) T and Emily celebrate the fortieth anniversary of their wedding-day. He gives her a posy of roses, syringa, and rosemary.

23 At Aldworth he works on 'The Church-Warden and the Curate', a humorous dialect poem based on what H. D. Rawnsley had told him in May of his own experience when he returned to Halton Holgate (where Drummond Rawnsley succeeded his father in 1861) after his ordination.

28 Finding some apple blossom and ripe strawberries, T observes, 'Miss Austen is not so wrong after all' (cf. *Emma*, xlii).

1–5 July T is in London with James Knowles, who takes him to Sir Andrew Clark's and to an oculist; T is certain that he is going blind. At the Knowleses' he meets several distinguished people, among them Lord Acton, Lady Pembroke, Lady Brownlow, the Gladstones, and Princess Mary, Duchess of Teck. He finds G persuasive on Home Rule for Ireland, but wishes next morning he had not agreed with him. On the 4th Hallam and he drive round Hyde Park in the morning, and see the Queen and Princess Louise, who bow to them; afterwards they visit Westminster Abbey to see Browning's grave.

August

6 (Wed) At Aldworth the Duchess of Albany lunches with the Ts in honour of the Poet Laureate's birthday, and thanks him for what he wrote on the Duke (cf. 29 Mar 1884). At her request he reads 'Guinevere'.

7 By this time the Bradleys and the second Lord Houghton have arrived.

Some time during the month, after hearing the story from F. W. Farrar, T begins his poem 'St Telemachus', the conclusion being based on a passage which F sent after his Aldworth visit.

23 T and Hallam are at Holmbury in Surrey, whence they can see Blackdown.

24 They drive to Wotton, where the diarist John Evelyn had lived. The Knowleses are 'as kind and hospitable as ever'.

October Norman Lockyer pays a visit, and talks much on Egypt and meteorites. T's mind is 'saturated with astronomy', he finds. On the 20th ET expects they will return to the Isle of Wight before the end of the month, unless the scarlet fever is 'very bad' there. (People from St Pancras have brought it, we learn from 'The Sanitary Authority', she writes.)

During the autumn hopes are raised – which prove delusive – that Irving will soon produce *The Foresters*.

November

5 (Wed) Hallam writes to G. L. Craik (of Macmillan's), asking if he has made the revision in 'The Leper's Bride',

and requesting him to send the new edition(?) of Mrs Craik's novels if the print is good, and 'put his name in it'.

9 ET informs Mr Craik that T will write to thank him for his 'valuable and beautiful gifts'.

16 T thanks Lockyer for his 'great hypothesis'. 'Almost (to parody Festus) thou persuadest me to be a "meteorist" ', he writes from Farringford.

26 It is extremely cold, and the damp has depressed T very much.

December A contract is signed for the production of *Becket*. (This comes to nothing in March 1891 with the death of Barrett, the American actor and signatory. A Christmas party arranged by Hallam's wife Audrey for their son Lionel is enjoyed by the Richard Wards and their five children, and by Lionel's grandparents as they sit in the Farringford ballroom with their servants, cottagers, and other guests.

1891

23 January T writes to Oliver Wendell Holmes, thanking him for the present of teacups which has at last arrived; they seem to have 'much of the old charm of The Breakfast Table'.

February T walks three miles up to the Beacon and back with Princess Louise, talking about Ireland and sculpture *inter alia*. Agnes Weld sends him a touching story ('vouched for by Mr H. Thornycroft') of a sculptor who died for the sake of his art. She was very interested to hear of T's race up to the Beacon with Princess Louise.

April Herbert Warren and his wife (from Oxford) visit T, who discusses Virgil with him. On the 8th Rudyard Kipling writes to Hallam, thanking T for his message, which is more than a decoration on the field to him. If there is any good in his (K's) verses, he adds, 'he knows more than I'.

June On the 9th Hallam and T begin their cruise along the south coast to Exmouth in Colonel Crozier's yacht *The Assegai*. From Exmouth they make their way north, partly by rail, to Exmoor valleys in the vicinity of Dulverton and Hawkridge, T beginning at the former place the hymn to the sun which concludes his 'Akbar's Dream'. (He recalls this Exmoor visit in 'June Bracken and Heather', designed as a dedication of his last volume of poetry to his wife.) On their way home they visit the ruins of Corfe Castle. Suddenly one day at Aldworth an American appears, saying that he has worked his way over in a cattle-ship in order to recite *Maud* to its author. T submits to the ordeal, and pays the reciter's return passage.

July He and Hallam are in London, where they stay with Knowles and with Mr Craik, and meet Aubrey de Vere and Lord Houghton.

6 August T spends his birthday quietly; he talks with de Vere about his earlier days. (During the month his letter appealing for further subscriptions for the Gordon Boys' Home appears in *The Daily Telegraph*.)

Summer The many guests at Aldworth include Lord and Lady Dufferin, the Leckys, Sir Daniel Wilson from Toronto University, the Dean of Westminster, the Henry Sidgwicks, and the poet Lewis Morris (a summer visitor in recent years). Jowett is too ill to make his usual visit.

September (late) Theodore Watts-Dunton finds T as poetically alert and active as he had been forty years earlier.

October

1 (Thurs) T writes a protest against Russian persecutions to the secretary of the Russo-Jewish committee.

8 Jowett, still seriously ill, writes to Hallam, thanking his father and mother for all their kindness to him; of all the houses where he has stayed, theirs has been the most like home to him. He thinks T should write 'a few hymns in a high strain' but 'nearer to the *familiar* thoughts of men than "In Memoriam" '.

(Later in the month (?) Augustin Daly visits Aldworth with the actress Ada Rehan to make arrangements for the production of *The Foresters* in New York.)

30 T is taken to Lymington, for Farringford, on a non-stop

train which has been specially commissioned for him, so much has his health deteriorated during the month.

November (early) Palgrave comes to see T, his first visit to Farringford since January 1863. On the 6th the American actress Ada Rehan writes. She has no time to spend a few days in the Ts' 'lovely country', but would so like to say goodbye to Lord and Lady T, before she sails on the 14th, if they could come and see her after one of her performances.

20 December T writes to the young poet William Watson to congratulate him on the poetry and patriotism of *Wordsworth's Grave*.

25 December On his way home with Wilfrid Ward (son and biographer of W. G. Ward), T climbs a difficult gate and runs down the hill, as he used to do in earlier years.

1892

6 January Hallam writes to Irving to secure the 'English rights' of *The Foresters* by arranging a 'nominal performance' to forestall Daly's production in New York.

During January Dr Hubert Parry stays at Farringford to hear T read 'The Lotos-Eaters', which he is setting to music. T's voice fails for the first time in reading this and the Wellington ode, which he would like set to music. As he had not been able to comply with the request of the Princess of Wales that he should write a poem on the coming of age of her son the Duke of Clarence, he feels obliged to act, though unwell, after the latter's death on the 14th, a few weeks after his engagement to Princess Mary of Teck, and writes 'The Death of the Duke of Clarence and Avondale'.

27 January The Montagu Butlers lunch at Farringford, and T recalls amusing events at Trinity College.

March
He reads 'The Passing of Arthur' to Lord Houghton and his sister Mrs Florence Henniker. 'Akbar's Dream' is nearing completion by the end of the month.

25 (Fri) *The Foresters* is produced by Daly in New York (the beginning of a long and successful run) with music by Sullivan. Ada Rehan, who plays the part of Maid Marian, writes to T; she is proud of her part and of the play's success.

31 Herbert Warren writes to say that he and his wife are coming on Tuesday for a week or so at Freshwater, and hopes to have the pleasure of seeing the Ts again. He finds *The Foresters* 'delightfully light and bright'. (He must have read it quickly; it was just being published.)

April

Early this month T has two or three talks with Warren on literary subjects.

19 (Tues) Bram Stoker, Irving's manager, makes the first of two calls at Farringford to discuss Irving's latest version of *Becket* for the stage.

26 James Beddoes, 'a poor old broken-down Farmer' of sixty, writes a well-penned letter of fifteen pages to T from Birmingham on his life and interest in T's poetry, and wonders whether T can find him a post as secretary or amanuensis to some gentleman.

May Palgrave comes to see T, and walks daily with him around his fields and farm and cottages.

June

Early this month the Duke of Connaught calls and discusses India with T.

5 (Sun) Lord Dufferin writes from Paris, earnestly hoping that he and his wife will have 'the infinite delight' of receiving Emily and T at Walmer in the later part of July; 'it would be such an inauguration as no Lord Warden ever had before'. (A little later in June, or about this time, Colonel Crozier lends his yacht again, and Hallam takes T on a cruise, first to Dartmouth, then to Guernsey, Sark, and Jersey, especially to see Frederick. They call at Torquay on their way back.)

29 T takes the sacrament in his study, only on the condition that (in words spoken by Cranmer in *Queen Mary*) it is 'not a mass' but 'a life-giving feast'.

30 The Ts leave for Aldworth.

July

4 (Mon) T writes to thank Edward Whymper for sending a copy of his *Maps to Travels Amongst the Great Andes*.

12 He and Hallam are staying with Mr Craik (2 Halkin Street West, London S.W.).

13 Norman Lockyer, Hallam writes to his mother, tells T that 500,000,000 suns have been counted. Yesterday they went to the Academy, where they liked Millais's *Halcyon Weather* and *Speedwell's Darling Blue*, and Herkomer's portrait of Lord Kelvin. The Dean of Westminster dines with them at Craik's.

14 They visit the Natural History Museum, and admire Darwin's statue presiding over the hall. They return to Aldworth tomorrow.

19 Palgrave, fulfilling T's wish that he should bring his daughters to see Aldworth, sees T for the last time.

8 August T is 'still suffering from gout in the throat and jaw', Emily informs her sister Anne Weld.

24 August T gives a reading of *Maud* for the last time, as he sits facing a window that overlooks the woods and yellow cornfields of the Sussex Weald.

(In the past few weeks, especially about the time of his birthday, he has received many visitors, including Mr Dakyns, Norman Lockyer, J. A. Symonds, and Edward Burne-Jones.)

September

ET discourages visitors. Hallam travels to Somersby, to tell his father how his old home (which is up for sale) looks. T's friends Benjamin Jowett and Lord Selborne come; he is no longer able to discuss or argue points of philosophy or religious uncertainty with the former. On his return Hallam sends for Dr Dabbs. Later Dakyns, Mr and Mrs Craik, and Mr and Mrs Bram Stoker call. T looks over proofs of his new volume of poetry with Craik, and discusses arrangements for the staging of *Becket* with Stoker. (The last poem T finished is 'The Dreamer'; among his latest are 'The Dawn', 'The Making of Man', and 'Faith'.)

26 (Mon) John Wordsworth, Bishop of Salisbury, writes to T. One of his sisters has Dora Wordsworth's album in which 'are four lines about the Eagle written in your own hand' (and others by T perhaps). He wishes to know if T has celebrated in

verse an incident in the life of King Arthur connected with his diocese, his carrying the cross in battle against the Saxons. A sonnet on the subject 'would be a great delight to us in Wilts and Dorset'.

28 Hallam takes his father to Haslemere in the morning (T's last drive). Sir Andrew Clark comes in response to a telegraph call.

October

2 (Sun) T's condition is much worse.

4 He is pleased to receive a telegram from the Queen.

5 Sir Andrew Clark comes from Christchurch. Dr Dabbs is in attendance as T rests during the night after farewell blessings to Emily and Hallam. The room and wide landscape are flooded with the light of a full moon.

6 T dies at 1.35 a.m., clasping the Shakespeare he had repeatedly called for during his last days. The news of his death reaches the Queen at Balmoral.

12 He is buried in Westminster Abbey. (Agnes Weld writes a full account of the proceedings for Emily, who is unable to attend.) The pall-bearers are the Duke of Argyll, Lord Dufferin, Lord Selborne, Lord Rosebery, Mr Jowett, Mr Lecky, Mr Froude, Lord Salisbury, Dr Montagu Butler, Sir James Paget, Lord Kelvin, and the United States Minister. The nave is lined by men of the Balaclava Light Brigade and the London Rifle Volunteers, and by boys of the Gordon Boys' Home. 'Crossing the Bar' and 'The Silent Voices' are sung, the latter to ET's music. The Duke of Argyll has seen nothing like it since the funeral of the Duke of Wellington. Thomas Hardy likes the music, but thinks the scene, for all its grandeur, 'less penetrating than a plain country interment would have been'. (Later Hallam receives a replica of Woolner's 1857 bust of T, and has it placed against the pillar near his grave.)

28 *The Death of Oenone, Akbar's Dream, and Other Poems* is published.

Becket at the Lyceum, with Henry Irving in the leading role, is a great success in 1893. For about four years Hallam is engaged in collecting and arranging papers and records for the Tennyson *Memoir*; he receives invaluable help from his mother. She dies at Aldworth on 10 August 1896. His *Alfred Lord Tennyson* is published in October 1897. He becomes Governor and Commander-in-Chief of South Australia (1899–1902) and Governor-General of Australia (1902–4).

Persons of Importance in Tennyson's Life

(The length of each of these sketches does not reflect comparative merit or importance. They are mainly intended to show how Tennyson's friends relate to him and his interests at different stages of his life. Those of whom sufficient is deemed to be given incidentally in the Chronology, and well-known authors such as Robert Browning, Thomas Carlyle, George Eliot, and Thackeray, are excluded.)

Joseph Williams Blakesley (1808–85) entered Corpus Christi, Cambridge, in 1827, became an Apostle, moved to Trinity, and won the Chancellor's Medal in 1831. T thought that his clear-headedness and integrity qualified him to be Lord Chancellor. At Trinity he became a fellow in 1831 and a tutor in 1834. He was one of the original members of the Sterling Club. Ordained early, he won much esteem as vicar of Ware (a college living) from 1845 to 1872; he was a canon of St Paul's from 1863, and Dean of Lincoln from 1872.

William Henry Brookfield (1809–74) was born in Sheffield, and entered Trinity College in 1829 as a sizar, to compensate his parents for having sacrificed his articles to a Leeds solicitor. A witty and amusing conversationalist and raconteur, he soon made many friends, including T and Arthur Hallam, Thackeray and A. W. Kinglake. Though not a member of the Apostles, he was on very good terms with most of them, and retained their friendship. He became President of the Cambridge Union. After graduating in 1832, and acting as tutor to Lord Lyttelton's eldest son, he was ordained to the curacy of Maltby (1834). An eloquent preacher, he moved to Southampton (1836), where he met his future wife, then to London (1838), where he served at St James's, Piccadilly, from 1840 to 1843, when he was given charge of St Luke's, Berwick Street. In 1841 he married Julia, daughter of Charles Elton and cousin of Arthur Hallam. He was an early member of the Sterling Club, a friend of the Carlyles, and a favourite at Lady Ashburton's parties.He became an Inspector of Schools in 1848.

Julia Margaret Cameron (1815–79), born in Calcutta, was the least beautiful of seven rich, eccentric, half-French Pattle sisters (one of whom married Henry Thoby Prinsep, a distinguished civil servant who returned from India in 1843, and leased Little Holland House in 1850). Her husband Charles Hay Cameron (1795–1880) was a fine scholar, who had been a legal member of the Supreme Council in Calcutta and a Royal Commissioner in Ceylon. She had a commanding personality, but was so kind and generous that T forgave her whatever inconvenience she caused him. She was, Agnes Weld wrote, 'almost the only woman outside his relations whom he called by her Christian name, and who called him in turn by his'. T was the attraction which brought the Camerons to the Isle of Wight in 1860. Profuse in her gifts and correspondence, she idolized the poet Henry Taylor even more. She took up photography with great enthusiasm in 1863. Such was her artistic perception that, although she was self-taught, she had great success in portraiture; her more allegorical subjects are outdated. The Cameron and Tennyson boys were about the same age, and on good terms, their activities including participation in plays. (Mrs Cameron had installed a theatre at Dimbola.)

Aubrey de Vere (1814–1902) was, like his father Sir Aubrey de Vere of Curragh Chase, County Limerick, a poet and dramatist. He was educated at Trinity College, Cambridge, and attracted by Wordsworth's poetry. He became a friend of Newman and Manning, and joined the Catholic Church in 1851. His prose writings are devoted chiefly to contemporary Irish affairs, literary criticism, and reminiscences. 'To my mind the friend of Tennyson's whose saintliness most completely had his sympathy was Aubrey de Vere', wrote Wilfrid Ward. Their friendship was 'almost lifelong, and showed Tennyson at his very best in conversation'.

Frederic William Farrar (1831–1903), son of a Bombay chaplain, was sent at the age of three to Aylesbury, where he remained under the care of two maiden aunts until he became a boarder at King William's College, the Isle of Man. (With these contrasting educational backgrounds in mind he wrote his first novel, *Eric, or Little by Little,* at Harrow in 1858.) During the time when his father was curate at St James's, Clerkenwell, Farrar attended King's College, London. A scholarship took him to Trinity, Cambridge, where he distinguished himself by winning one offered by Trinity, as well as the Chancellor's Medal for English verse. He became a member of the Apostles, and graduated in 1854. He taught first at Marlborough, then at Harrow, where he served under Montagu Butler. Ordained at an early age, he became the Queen's chaplain in 1869, and head of Marlborough in 1871. In 1876 he was made a canon of Westminster; in 1883, archdeacon. Influenced by F. D. Maurice's teaching at King's College, his sermons in the Abbey against eternal punishment created controversy and offence. Such broad views hindered his promotion until 1895, when he was appointed Dean of Canterbury. He wrote on philology and grammar, education, the classics, and much on religious subjects.

Edward FitzGerald (1809–83) was born in Suffolk of Irish parents, and sent to Bury St Edmunds Grammar School, where his friendships with Spedding, Kemble, and W. B. Donne began. He entered Trinity College, Cambridge, in 1826 and left with a pass degree in 1830, chief among his friends being Thackeray, W. H. Thompson, and Charles Merivale. With an annual allowance of £300 he rented lodgings in London, and led a carefree bachelor life. From 1837 he lived most of his time in the Woodbridge area of Suffolk, becoming closely acquainted with the Quaker poet Bernard Barton, George Crabbe (son of the poet), and E. B. Cowell of Ipswich, whose zeal for languages led him to read Spanish and Persian. After minor publications, he produced *Six Dramas of Calderón* (1853) and a poetical version of Omar Khayyám's *Rubáiyát* (1859), which remained unsold and almost unknown until 1861, when it was put out for sale in the publisher's penny-box and brought to the notice of D. G. Rossetti and Swinburne, after which its heterodox fame spread steadily. FitzGerald later translated plays by Aeschylus and Sophocles. A great reader and letter-writer, he usually showed sound literary judgment, but, after the 1842 volumes (which he made it his business to see published), his attitude to T's new publications was more critical and indifferent, as he showed in his letters, particularly to Frederick T; he became more interested in the poetry of Crabbe. Fitz loved a flow of correspondence, and

T rarely replied; to spare ET, he reduced his Tennyson letters to about two a year. Yet, when Fitz and T met briefly in 1876, reservations were soon dispelled, and the old warmth of friendship revived.

John Forster (1812–76), journalist, historian, and biographer, began writing political articles in *The Examiner* in 1833. After being editor successively of *The Foreign Quarterly Review*, *The Daily News*,and *The Examiner* (1847–56), he wrote several important studies, particularly on the Commonwealth period. His biography of Goldsmith (1848) was widely read, but he is best remembered for *The Life of Charles Dickens* (1872–4). He was a tireless student and most devoted friend. His books, manuscripts, and pictures were left to the Victoria and Albert Museum.

James Anthony Froude, historian (1818–94), son of the Archdeacon of Totnes, Devon, was educated at Westminster School and Oxford, where he won the Chancellor's English prize for his essay 'The Influence of Political Economy on the Moral and Social Welfare of the Nation'. He became a fellow of Exeter College in 1842, and a deacon in 1844, while he was still influenced by Newman. His Tractarianism undermined by Carlyle's writings, he lost both his fellowship and the headship of a school in Tasmania. After writing for *The Westminster Review* and *Fraser's Magazine* (the second of which he edited from 1860 to 1874) he turned principally for about twenty years to his *History of England from the Fall of Cardinal Wolsey to the Spanish Armada*, a subject chosen for its controversial religious interest, and an influence on T's *Queen Mary*. Froude's *The English in Ireland* (1871–4) was equally polemical and Carlylean in its ethical principles. His biography of Carlyle (1882–4) excited even greater controversy. He was a master of narrative style who regarded history as 'a voice for ever sounding across the centuries the laws of right and wrong'. A lover of the sea from the time of his Devonian youth, he died at Salcombe, after being two years Regius Professor of History at Oxford.

William Ewart Gladstone, Liberal statesman (1809–98), was the son of a Liverpool merchant, and educated at Eton and Christ Church, Oxford. As a Conservative M.P., he served under Robert Peel. The Corn Law agitation made him realize the inequities of the social system. He was Chancellor of the Exchequer in the Coalition Ministry, and again under Palmerston. Under Lord Russell he became leader of the House of Commons. The serious state of Ireland and the Fenian insurrection brought the Liberals to power with Gladstone as Prime Minister in 1868; a number of reforms followed in England and Ireland. After Disraeli had been in office, Gladstone returned to power in 1880. He was returned again in 1886, after a short-lived Conservative ministry under Lord Salisbury. He believed in Home Rule for Ireland, but was defeated on this question, yet returned again to office in 1892. After his Home Rule bill had been rejected by the House of Lords, old age made him retire in 1894. He died at Hawarden, and was buried in Westminster Abbey.

Arthur Henry Hallam (1811–33), son of Henry Hallam and of Julia, daughter of Sir Abraham Elton of Clevedon Court, was, like his father, extremely precocious. At the age of nine he read French and Latin fluently, and had written tragedies in prose and verse. The outstanding scholar at Eton, where Gladstone was his greatest friend, he suffered severely from headaches and participated little in school games. When he left in 1827 he spent seven or eight months in Italy, becoming acquainted with great Italian art and literature, Dante especially. He wrote both Italian and English verse. In Rome he and his school friend Milnes Gaskell fancied they were in love with Anne Wintour (ten years Arthur's senior). Thinking it sensible to separate him from Milnes Gaskell and Gladstone, Henry Hallam sent his son to Cambridge. Arthur brought with him the enthusiasm for Keats and Shelley which had been fostered in Rome. Poetry drew him to T in 1829, and he was very active in the publication and promotion of *Poems, Chiefly Lyrical* (1830). His father's ambitious concentration on his welfare was undoubtedly spurred by the loss of all his elder sons; his main hope was destroyed by Arthur's death in 1833.

Henry Hallam, Whig historian (1777–1859), was the son of John Hallam, Canon of Windsor, later Dean of Bristol. A precocious child, who read much at four and composed sonnets when he was ten, he was educated at Eton and Christ Church, Oxford. Called to the bar, he practised on the Oxford circuit. He married Julia, Sir Abraham Elton's daughter, in 1807. Independence enabled him to pursue his historical interests. His work on Europe in the Middle

Ages brought him distinction; it was followed by a constitutional history of England and an introduction to European literature. He had many friends, but his life was saddened by the loss of his children; of the eleven only four grew up, and of these all but one, Julia, died young.

Benjamin Jowett (1817–93) was educated at St Paul's School and Balliol, Oxford, where, after winning classical distinctions, he was made a fellow and tutor. From 1855 he was Regius Professor of Greek. His Broad Church views and his contribution to *Essays and Reviews* (1860) brought him into disfavour and hampered his promotion. He was popular with his students and, after becoming Master of Balliol in 1870, his liberal influence permeated the college. He was Vice-Chancellor of the University from 1882 to 1886. Today he is remembered most for his translation and editing of Plato's dialogues.

John Mitchell Kemble (1807–57), a member of a famous stage family, was remembered at Bury St Edmunds Grammar School for his acting and declamation. He entered Trinity, Cambridge, in 1825, but neglected his studies for general reading and activities in which he could express his lively personality. He was a member of the Apostles. After a period in Germany and participation in the Spanish revolutionary cause he returned to take a degree in order to gain a living which would give him time to continue the philological studies he had begun in Germany. He edited *The British and Foreign Review* from 1835 to 1844, and succeeded his father as Examiner of Plays in 1840. Pre-eminently he became an Anglo-Saxon scholar, the most important of his publications being the unfinished *History of the Saxons in England*. He died of pneumonia in Dublin, where he was to lecture to the Royal Academy.

Edward Lear (1812–88), artist, author, traveller (and talented musician), is best remembered for his limericks and lyrical 'nonsense' verse. He was a draughtsman for the Zoological Society. His enthusiasm for landscape-painting led the Earl of Derby to send him to Italy and Greece, but his travels extended to India. His later years were spent in Italy. In the spring of 1849 he was accompanied by Franklin Lushington, whom he had met in Malta; theirs was a friendship of opposites. T found him tiring;

ET pitied him, and he was grateful. He named his Italian home, at San Remo, Villa Tennyson.

William Edward Hartpole Lecky (1838–1903), born in Dublin and educated for the Irish Church, soon decided to become a historian. He wrote on the spirit of rationalism in Europe, and on European morals from Augustus to Charlemagne. His principal work is a history of England in the eighteenth century. Although he had genuine Irish sympathies, he opposed Home Rule. He produced a volume of poems in 1891.

Joseph Norman Lockyer, English astronomer (1836–1920), detected helium in the sun's chromosphere by daylight (1868). He was made a fellow of the Royal Society in 1869, and a lecturer on astronomy at South Kensington in 1870. He headed eclipse expeditions, edited *Nature* (which he and Alexander Macmillan founded in 1869), wrote works on astronomy, solar chemistry and physics, and the meteoritic hypothesis, and was knighted in 1897.

Edmund Law Lushington (1811–93) was educated at Charterhouse and at Trinity, Cambridge, where he became an Apostle, won the Chancellor's Classic Medal in 1832, and was elected to a fellowship in 1834. He was appointed Professor of Greek at Glasgow University in 1838, a position he occupied until 1875. Friendships between Lushingtons and Tennysons grew when the latter lived at Boxley, near Maidstone. Edmund married T's sister Cecilia, and T stayed at Park House, the Lushingtons' home, frequently.

Franklin Lushington (1823–1901), another of the Park House family, was educated at Rugby and Trinity, Cambridge. A barrister, he became a member of the Supreme Council of Justice in the Ionian Islands (1855–8). He was a great friend of Edward Lear, and accepted the guardianship of T's two sons.

Henry Lushington (1812–55), second son of Edmund Henry Lushington of Park House, was head boy at Charterhouse at the age of fifteen. He entered Trinity College, Cambridge, in 1829, lost two years through ill-health, won the Porson Prize for Greek iambics in 1832 and 1833, and graduated as Senior Optime in 1834. Like Edmund, he was an Apostle who became a fellow of Trinity. A student of the Inner Temple, he was made a barrister in 1840, but rarely practised. His literary memory was prodigious, especially with reference to Shakespeare, Carlyle's *French Revolution*, and the poems of T, who regarded his criticism with high esteem,and dedicated *The Princess* to him. Lord Grey made him Chief Secretary to the Government of Malta in 1847. He fell seriously ill in 1855. On his way home he was met in the south of France by his best friend G. S. Venables, who escorted him to Paris, where he died.

John Frederick Denison Maurice (1805–72), son of a Unitarian minister, studied at Trinity College and Trinity Hall, Cambridge, but, being a dissenter, left without a degree in 1827, after helping to found the Apostles. His novel *Eustace Conway* appeared in 1834. Influenced by Coleridge's thought, he took orders in the Church of England, and became a chaplain, first to Guy's Hospital, then to Lincoln's Inn (1841–60). In 1840 he was appointed to a professorship of literature at King's College, London; later, to the professorship of theology, a post he lost in 1853, when his views on eternal punishment in *Theological Essays* were deemed unacceptably heterodox. From 1866 he was Professor of Moral Philosophy at Cambridge. He was the mainspring of the Christian Socialist movement, and founder of the Working Men's College and the Queen's College for Women, at both of which he taught.

Charles Merivale (1808–93) studied at Harrow and St John's, Cambridge, where he displayed all-round excellence as a student, cricketer, oarsman, Apostle, and prize poet. He took orders in 1833, and was a fellow and tutor at St John's until 1849. While a rector in Essex he wrote *A History of the Romans under the Empire* (1850–62). He was Dean of Ely from 1869 until his death. His translation of Homer's *Iliad* appeared in 1878.

Richard Monckton Milnes (1809–85), a descendant of Wakefield woollen manufacturers, was born at Fryston Hall near Pontefract, and educated privately before entering Trinity College, Cambridge, in 1827; he and T were elected Apostles on the same day. He was M.P. for Pontefract from 1837 until he became Lord Houghton in 1863. His travels in Europe, the Middle East, and the United States made him many friends, especially in France. His political ambitions were frustrated, probably because he was more candid than discreet in expressing his liberal views. His verse enhanced his reputation, and he had considerable influence, playing an important part in the choice of T as Poet Laureate, and doing much to promote Swinburne. His qualities remained much as AH noted in December 1829: witty, frank, light-humoured, unruffled in temper, saucy but so consistently kind that one ignored 'the extravaganzas of his always random conversation', which was less superficial than it might at first have seemed. He was excellently qualified to follow Samuel Rogers in the entertainment of friends and eminent people, which he did at Fryston Hall, and at London breakfast parties, first at 26 Pall Mall, then, after his marriage in 1851 to the Honourable Annabella Crewe, at 16 Upper Brook Street. His most permanent contribution to literature probably derives from his *Life, Letters and Literary Remains of John Keats* (1848) and his subsequent editions of Keats's poetry.

Francis Turner Palgrave (1824–97), poet and critic, son of the historian Sir Francis Palgrave (*né* Cohen), attended Charterhouse, won a scholarship at Balliol, and became assistant secretary to Gladstone before gaining a first in classics in 1847. He was made a fellow of Exeter College, Oxford. From 1850 to 1855, as long as it existed, he was vice-principal of Kneller Hall, a training-college for schoolmasters not far from Chapel House, Twickenham. With T he discussed inclusions for his famous anthology *The Golden Treasury of English Lyrics* (1861). He married Cecil Milnes-Gaskell, whom he met at Fryston Hall in the summer, at the end of 1862. He was successively private secretary to Lord Granville, official in the Education Department, and Professor of Poetry at Oxford (1886–95).

William Gifford Palgrave (1826–88), brother of the above, graduated at Oxford, and spent a period in India. He became a Jesuit, studied at Rome, and undertook missionary work in Syria, where he narrowly escaped the massacre of Christians by the Druzes in 1860. In 1862–3, on behalf of Napoleon III, he made the daring expedition which he describes in *Narrative of a Year's Journey through Central and Eastern Arabia*. After severing connections with the Jesuits, he entered the diplomatic service, and was sent to Abyssinia in 1865. Duties as British consul took him to many parts of the world, including Trebizond (Turkey),

St Thomas (West Indies), Bulgaria, and Bangkok. He died at Montevideo, Uruguay.

Coventry Patmore (1823–96), privately educated, drifted into poetry and became associated with the Pre-Raphaelites. Monckton Milnes helped him to obtain a post as assistant librarian at the British Museum. His most famous poem, *The Angel in the House*, inspired by his first wife, who died in 1862, was greeted enthusiastically and became very popular. Influenced by the lady who became his second wife, and brought him wealth, Patmore turned Catholic and retired to Sussex, finally settling at Hastings, where, after her death, he built a fine Catholic church. His other notable publication is *The Unknown Eros* (1877), a collection of odes combining fervent devotion with Catholic mysticism.

William Frederick Pollock (1815–88), jurist and author, was educated at St Paul's School and at Trinity, Cambridge, where he graduated in 1836. At the Inner Temple he was called to the bar in 1838. After working on the northern circuit, he became a Master of the Court of Exchequer in 1846, and Queen's Remembrancer in 1874. He succeeded his father (1st Baronet in 1866) as 2nd Baronet in 1870; his home was in Montagu Square. Pollock made and maintained many friendships among notabilities, but devoted time to cultural pursuits. He translated Dante's *Divina Commedia*; edited the *Reminiscences* of his friend the actor William Macready, with selections from his diaries and letters; and preserved a valuable, concise, and entertaining record of his own life and friendships in *Personal Remembrances* (1887).

Sir John Simeon (1815–70) was a Roman Catholic who represented the Isle of Wight in Parliament from 1847 to 1851 and from 1865 to 1870. He was a good landlord, master of the hunt, and scholarly. T, who described him as the prince of courtesy, was introduced to Simeon, possibly as early as January 1850, by Carlyle, at Bath House, the Ashburtons' London residence. Their friendship began in July 1854.

James Spedding (1808–81) was one of Edward FitzGerald's friends at Bury St Edmunds Grammar School, though his home was in the Lake District, where his father had been Wordsworth's friend at Hawkshead Grammar School. In 1827 he entered Trinity

College, Cambridge. An Apostle, on good terms with the Ts, AH, Monckton Milnes, and many others, he showed a maturity of judgment which led T and Fitz to describe him as the wisest man they knew. He was a scholar who lacked 'the smartness required for success in examinations'. Having failed to secure a fellowship at Trinity, he took a temporary post in the Colonial Office from 1835 to 1841. For more than thirty years he made the works of Lord Bacon his major study; there were few interruptions. He was secretary to Lord Ashburton's mission to the United States in 1842, and to the Civil Service Commission when it was instituted in 1855. He rejected the office of permanent under-secretary for the colonies at £2000 p.a. in 1847, a professorship of modern history at Cambridge in 1869, and an honorary degree in 1874. The works of Bacon were published from 1857 to 1859; his life and letters, from 1861 to 1874. Spedding's editing was exceptionally thorough, and notable for its exposure of Macaulay's misrepresentations. He remained single, occupying rooms in Lincoln's Inn Fields until 1867, after which he lived with relatives in Westbourne Terrace. It was typical of his generous-mindedness that he exonerated the unfortunate cabman who caused his fatal injuries.

Stephen Spring Rice (1814–65), of Bury St Edmunds Grammar School and Trinity, Cambridge, was Aubrey de Vere's first cousin. He was a member of the Apostles and later of the Sterling Club. After being made private secretary to his father (Chancellor of the Exchequer, made Baron Monteagle in 1839) he became Commissioner of Customs (1838–56) and deputy chairman of the Board of Customs, from which he retired in 1859 owing to ill-health. He died at sea while returning from Gibraltar. Two of his sisters married Marshalls (one, J. G. Marshall of Tent Lodge, Coniston). His father, Lord Monteagle of Mount Trenchard, County Limerick, married the eldest sister of his sons-in-law in 1841, after losing his first wife. Pollock described Stephen as 'one of the most gifted and charming of men'.

John Sterling (1806–44) was born at Kames Castle, Bute, and sent to school (like Coleridge, whose thought was to influence him strongly) at Christ's Hospital. After attending Glasgow University, he entered Trinity College in 1824, and was one of the founders of the Apostles. With others he acquired *The Athenaeum* in 1828, he and F. D. Maurice assuming its main management for half a year. His novel *Arthur Coningsby* came out in 1833, when he was ordained; in 1834–5 he served as his former tutor Julius Charles Hare's curate at Herstmonceux. Sterling had a vigorous personality, and could be vehemently eloquent in the denunciation of abuses. His disastrous espousal of the 1830 Spanish insurrectionary movement, with the death of his cousin Boyd, cast a shadow over the rest of his life. His curacy was an aberration, for he could not subscribe to the Thirty-Nine Articles. In 1838 he founded the London club which was subsequently named in his honour. His health broke down repeatedly, but his integrity and example had such appeal that his countryman Carlyle helped to preserve his memory in *The Life of John Sterling*.

Henry Taylor (1800–86), son of a cultured Durham gentleman–farmer, became a clerk in the Colonial Office, where he remained forty-eight years. He wrote four tragedies in a poetical style (rather than the Shakespearian, which was claimed for them), the second, *Philip van Artevelde* (1834), being an immediate success, and two volumes of poetry. His *Autobiography* (1885) contains interesting sketches of contemporaries. For his writing he was awarded a doctorate by Oxford in 1862; for his public work he was knighted in 1869.

Tom Taylor (1817–80) studied with distinction at Glasgow University and Trinity College, Cambridge, where he became a fellow. After being Professor of English at University College, London, he was called to the bar, and appointed to the Board of Health, of which he was secretary from 1854 until retirement. His literary work (chiefly dramatic) was usually done before breakfast. Over a hundred works, original or adapted, were written by him for the stage, and many of them were highly successful. He edited the autobiographies of B. R. Haydon and C. R. Leslie, and became editor of *Punch* in 1874.

Robert John Tennant (1809–42) entered Trinity, Cambridge, from Christ's Hospital in 1827, became an Apostle, and graduated in 1831. After teaching briefly at London University School, he became second master at Blackheath School. In 1834 he fell in love with Cecilia Tennyson. Entering the Church, he worked, like Sterling, as J. C. Hare's curate at Herstmonceux. His later years were spent in Florence as chaplain to the British embassy.

John Tyndall (1820–93), born in Ireland and largely self-educated, taught physics in England and Germany, and became a professor at the Royal Institution in 1854. A visit to the Alps with T. H. Huxley led to their joint publication on glaciers. Tyndall researched on heat radiation and atmospheric acoustics, and wrote lucidly in scientific journals to make scientific truths widely known. His work won him many honours, at home and abroad.

George Stovin Venables (1810–88), son of the Archdeacon of Carmarthen, was a contemporary of Thackeray at Charterhouse, entered Jesus College, Cambridge, in 1829, and won the Chancellor's Gold Medal in 1831 for a poem on the North-West Passage. Tall, handsome, and charming, he became a fellow and tutor at Jesus before reading law at the Inner Temple, where he was called to the bar in 1836. After working on the Oxford circuit, he turned to parliamentary practice. In 1863 he became a Queen's counsel. As an anonymous journalist he maintained a clear, vigorous style, and high standards in political thought. He contributed frequently to *The Saturday Review*, for the first number of which he wrote the first leading article. Annually, for twenty-five years in succession, he surveyed events for *The Times*. He was an Apostle, a member of the Sterling Club, and T's lifelong friend.

William George Ward (1812–82), educated at Winchester College and Christ Church, Oxford, became a fellow and tutor at Balliol. He lectured in mathematics and logic. Although attracted by the rationalism of J. S. Mill and Auguste Comte, he fell under the influence of Newman. His Tractarian publications led to the loss of his lectureship and fellowship. He married, became a Catholic, and received a Ph.D. from the Pope. He edited *The Dublin Review* from 1863 to 1878. Although theologically narrow and rigid, and a believer in papal infallibility, he was very generous in his philosophical outlook, and had an engaging personality. One of the first members of the Metaphysical Society in 1869, he was its President in 1870.

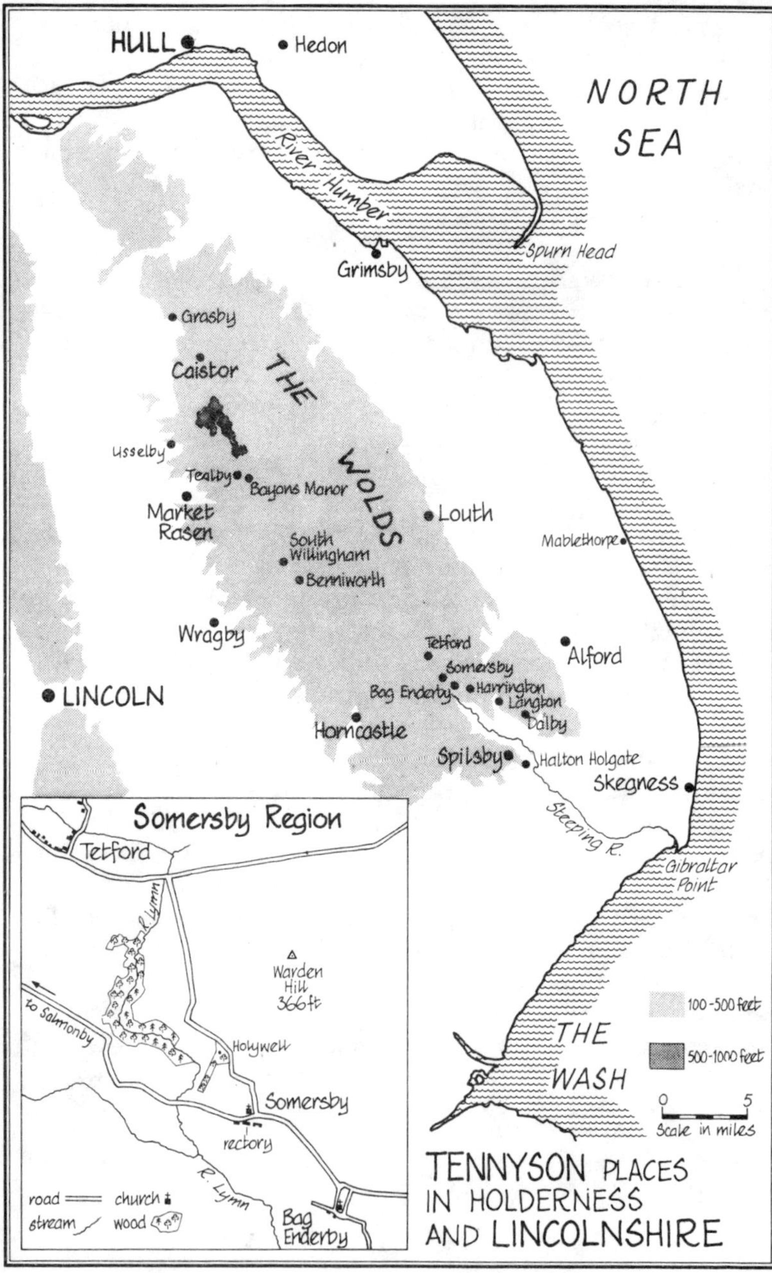

Map 1 Tennyson places in Holderness and Lincolnshire

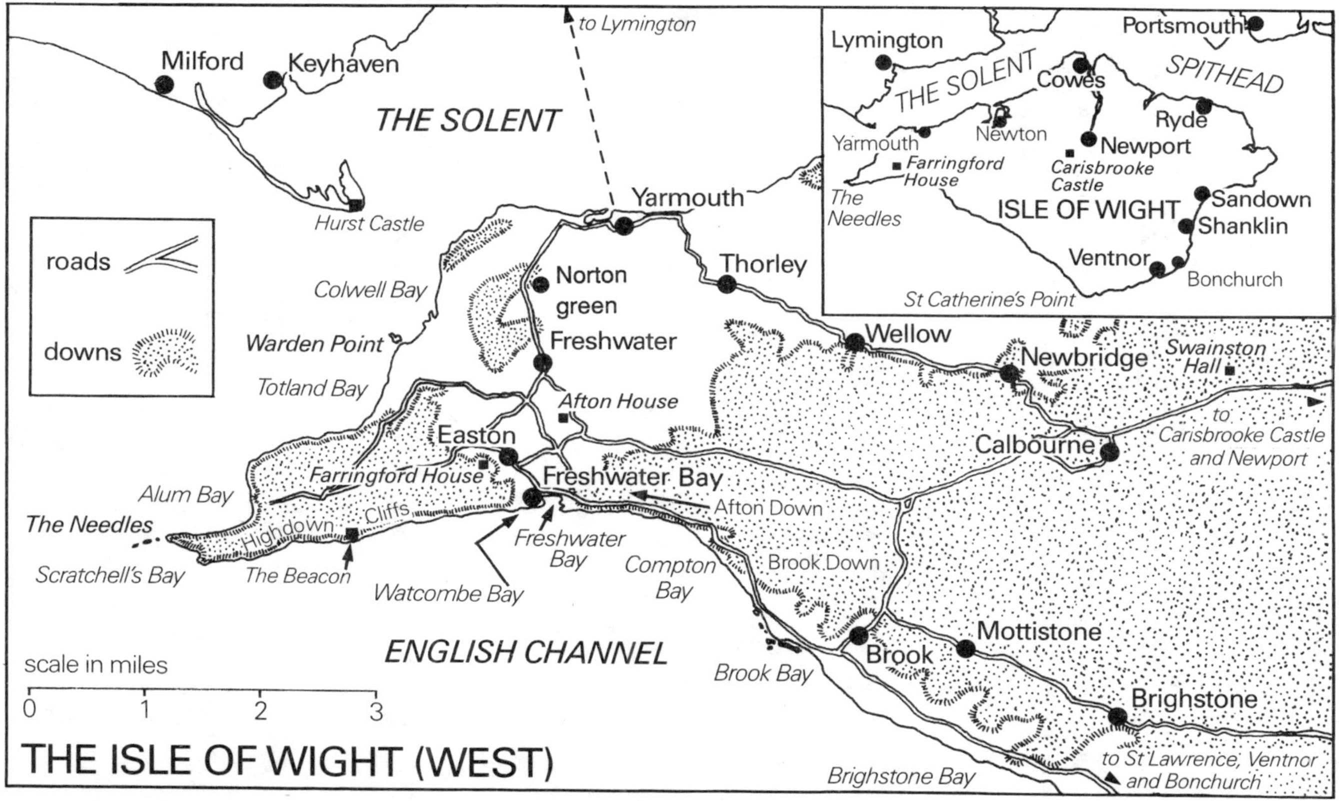
THE ISLE OF WIGHT (WEST)
scale in miles
0
1
2
3
roads
downs
Milford
Keyhaven
THE SOLENT
to Lymington
Hurst Castle
Yarmouth
Thorley
Colwell Bay
Warden Point
Totland Bay
Norton
green
Freshwater
Afton House
Easton
Farringford House
Freshwater Bay
Afton Down
Alum Bay
The Needles
Highdown
Cliffs
The Beacon
Scratchell's Bay
Watcombe Bay
Freshwater
Bay
Compton
Bay
Brook Down
ENGLISH CHANNEL
Brook Bay
Brook
Mottistone
Brighstone
Brighstone Bay
to St Lawrence, Ventnor
and Bonchurch
Wellow
Newbridge
Swainston
Hall
Calbourne
to
Carisbrooke Castle
and Newport
Lymington
Portsmouth
THE SOLENT
Cowes
SPITHEAD
Ryde
Yarmouth
Newton
Newport
Farringford
House
Carisbrooke
Castle
The
Needles
ISLE OF WIGHT
Sandown
Shanklin
Ventnor
Bonchurch
St Catherine's Point

Bibliography

Only the most important sources for *A Tennyson Chronology* are given below. Books such as Charles Morgan, *The House of Macmillan*, Macmillan, London, 1943, and Derek Hudson, *Munby: Man of Two Worlds*, Murray, London, 1972, which have contributed only to a very small extent, have been excluded on the assumption that a select list will provide the most helpful guidance for the reader.

A. Tennyson Letters and Diaries

Cecil Y. Lang and Edgar F. Shannon (eds), *The Letters of Alfred Lord Tennyson*, vol. I (1821–50), Harvard University Press, Cambridge, Mass., 1981; vol. II (1851–70), Clarendon Press, Oxford, 1987; vol. III to follow.

Hope Dyson and Charles Tennyson (eds), *Dear and Honoured Lady*, Macmillan, London, 1969.

James O. Hoge (ed.), *The Letters of Emily Lady Tennyson* (a selection), Pennsylvania State University Press, University Park and London, 1974.

James O. Hoge (ed.), *Lady Tennyson's Journal*, University Press of Virginia, Charlottesville, 1981.

Richard J. Hutchings and Brian Hinton (eds), *The Farringford Journal of Emily Tennyson, 1853–1864*, Isle of Wight County Press, Newport, 1986.

B. Letters and Records by Tennyson's Contemporaries

Jack Kolb (ed.), *The Letters of Arthur Henry Hallam*, Ohio State University Press, Columbus, 1981.

A. M. and A. B. Terhune (eds), *The Letters of Edward FitzGerald* (4 vols), Princeton University Press, 1980.

William Allingham's Diary (introduction by Geoffrey Grigson), Centaur Press, Fontwell, Sussex, 1967.

Hallam, Lord Tennyson (ed.), *Tennyson and His Friends*, Macmillan, London, 1911.
Sir Frederick Pollock, *Personal Remembrances* (2 vols), Macmillan, London, 1887.

Other volumes have been consulted and drawn from, including various collections of letters by both Thomas and Jane Carlyle, the letters of Edward Lear, Arthur Hugh Clough (2 vols, ed. F. L. Mulhauser, Clarendon Press, Oxford, 1957), 'Lewis Carroll' (2 vols, ed. Morton N. Cohen, Macmillan, London, 1979), George Eliot (7 vols, ed. Gordon Haight, Yale University Press, New Haven and Oxford University Press, Oxford, 1954 and 1957), reminiscences by Lady Ritchie (*née* Anne Thackeray), and recollections by Audrey Tennyson of talks with her father-in-law (*Journal of English and Germanic Philology*, 1978).

C. Biographies

Hallam Tennyson, *Alfred Lord Tennyson: A Memoir* (2 vols), Macmillan, London and New York, 1897.
Charles Tennyson, *Alfred Tennyson*, Macmillan, London, 1949.
Robert B. Martin, *Tennyson: The Unquiet Heart*, Clarendon Press, Oxford, and Oxford University Press, New York, 1980.

Among other biographical works, including those on Richard Monckton Milnes, the following have been most useful:

Charles and Frances Brookfield, *Mrs. Brookfield and Her Circle*, Pitman, London, 1905.
Gordon Haight, *George Eliot: A Biography*, Oxford University Press, New York and Oxford, 1968.
Gwenllian F. Palgrave, *Francis Turner Palgrave*, Longman, Green, and Co., London, 1899.
H. D. Rawnsley, *Memories of the Tennysons*, Maclehose, Glasgow, 1900.
Wilfrid Ward, *Aubrey de Vere*, Longman, Green, and Co., London, 1904.
Amy Woolner, *Thomas Woolner: His Life in Letters*, Chapman and Hall, London, 1917.

D. Miscellaneous

June Steffensen Hagen, *Tennyson and His Publishers*, Macmillan, London, 1979.

Helmut Gernsheim, *Julia Margaret Cameron*, Gordon Fraser, London, 1975.

Christopher Ricks (ed.), *The Poems of Tennyson*, Longman, Green, and Co., London, 1969 (2nd edition in 3 vols, 1987). Contains much chronological detail.

Norman Page, *Tennyson: Interviews and Recollections*, Macmillan, London, 1983. Includes useful chronological excerpts.

General Index

Index to Tennyson's Poems and Plays